Jukebox Empire

JUKEBOX EMPIRE
The Mob and the Dark Side of the American Dream

DAVID RABINOVITCH

ROWMAN & LITTLEFIELD
Lanham • Boulder • New York • London

Published by Rowman & Littlefield
An imprint of The Rowman & Littlefield Publishing Group, Inc.
4501 Forbes Boulevard, Suite 200, Lanham, Maryland 20706
www.rowman.com

86-90 Paul Street, London EC2A 4NE

Distributed by NATIONAL BOOK NETWORK

British Library Cataloguing in Publication Information available

Library of Congress Cataloging-in-Publication Data
Names: Rabinovitch, John David, author.
Title: Jukebox empire : the mob and the dark side of the American dream / David Rabinovitch.
Description: Lanham, Maryland : Rowman & Littlefield Publishers, [2023] | Includes bibliographical references and index.
Identifiers: LCCN 2022047514 (print) | LCCN 2022047515 (ebook) | ISBN 9781538172599 (cloth) | ISBN 9781538172605 (ebook)
Subjects: LCSH: Bank robberies--United States. | Money laundering--United States.
Classification: LCC HV6658 .R33 2023 (print) | LCC HV6658 (ebook) | DDC 364.15/520973--dc23/eng/20230404
LC record available at https://lccn.loc.gov/2022047514
LC ebook record available at https://lccn.loc.gov/2022047515

♾️™ The paper used in this publication meets the minimum requirements of American National Standard for Information Sciences—Permanence of Paper for Printed Library Materials, ANSI/NISO Z39.48-1992.

Contents

Illustrations

Cast of Characters

CAPEHART, HOMER EARL (1897–1979). A wheeler-dealer whose career begins selling popcorn wagons. Acquiring patents from inventors, Capehart packages the rights to the WurliTzer Corporation and turns it into the biggest jukebox manufacturer in the United States. As WurliTzer's general manager, he turns to racketeers for distribution. They muscle out the competition, jukebox production increases tenfold, and *Fortune* describes Capehart as "the greatest salesman America has ever produced." Capehart cashes out to finance a political campaign. A conservative Republican, he is elected to the U.S. Senate, a position from which he can fend off attempts to investigate the coin machine industry.

CHAVIANO, OLGA (1925–2003). The Cuban spitfire, a rumba dancer, singer, entertainer, Cuban movie star, and the headliner at Havana's big casinos, the Sans Souci, and the Tropicana. Married to casino owner Norman Rothman, she is detained by order of Fidel Castro but escapes Cuba in 1966. She restarts her career in the United States with a spectacular show costarring her son Faustino Rothman.

COTRONI, GIUSEPPE "PEP" (1920–1979). Born in Reggio Calabria on the Italian boot, Cotroni grew up on the ruthless streets of Montreal's Little Italy. Described in his file at the U.S. Bureau of Narcotics Investigation as "a terrorist and a vicious hoodlum."[1] With his brother Vicenzo, aka "Vic the Egg," he initiates the French Connection and controls the biggest heroin syndicate in North America. He attends the Mafia summit at Apalachin, New York, in 1957, but escapes the FBI across the border into Quebec.

FILBEN, WILLIAM (1899–1940). A hard-drinking Irish American, he makes coin-operated radios, which he sells to hotels and bars. A tinkerer and inventor, Filben designs a jukebox mechanism that can play thirty records. He dreams of wealth but dies of a heart attack, leaving the rights to his invention to his widow and children.

GORMAN, RICHARD (1912–1995). Built like a fullback, the Chicago beat cop earns a law degree at night. He gets a position as a junior prosecutor in the federal district attorney's office, where many prosecutors are on the take. Gorman hangs out his shingle and builds a lucrative practice defending syndicate bosses on federal charges, notably representing Teamsters Union president James Hoffa in a land-fraud case. Considered brilliant at finding legal loopholes, he is indicted for conspiracy to bribe a juror and later convicted of income tax evasion.

KENNEDY, ROBERT F. (1925–1968). In 1958, JFK's younger brother is out to make a name for himself as chief counsel for a U.S. Senate committee investigating racketeering in the coin machine industry. Tough, competitive, suspicious, and tightly wound, the charismatic Kennedy is lightning in a cathode ray tube. Kennedy subpoenas a parade of powerful racketeers to testify under the television lights in highly charged interrogations.

LANSKY, MEYER (1902–1983). The financial genius who strategizes the transition of organized crime into legitimate businesses. Lansky, who will pioneer casino operations in Havana, first runs jukebox routes as an operator in Florida in the 1930s. When the WurliTzer Company cannot make sales in the New York market, it turns to Lansky, who becomes the WurliTzer franchisee in 1943 and soon takes control of the market.

MANION, DONALD (1928–2011). Joined the U.S. Navy, rose to lieutenant on a destroyer in the Korean War. Decorated five times for bravery, the fair-haired blue-eyed war hero returns to marry his high school sweetheart and attends law school on the GI Bill. He gets his dream job in the district attorney's office, where he is on a mission to clean up crime syndicates. Prosecuting the largest money-laundering scheme in history offers the opportunity of a lifetime.

MANNARINO, SAM (1902–1967). A graduate of the Sicilian Mafia's school for survival, head of the Pittsburgh family of La Cosa Nostra, he runs an empire of coin-ops, jukes and cigarette machines, trucking, chemicals, billiard parlors, nightclubs, and other rackets. Beady-eyed, always figuring the angle. Charming like a snake. From his headquarters in a salvage yard, Mannarino schemes to invest the millions he harvests from the jukeboxes into manufacturing them.

MARGIOTTI, CHARLES (1891–1956). A tall, portly, bespectacled man with a patrician profile and the oratorical skills of a Roman senator. Margiotti successfully prosecutes the first woman to go to the electric chair in Pennsylvania and becomes the first Italian American to hold the office of attorney general of that state. Crossing the bar to the defense, he achieves acquittals for 149 accused murderers. Consigliere to the Mannarino brothers, he represents their interests in the Pittsburgh Pirates and Filben Manufacturing.

MEROLA, JOSEPH RAYMOND (1925–2004). A U.S. Marine pilot who turned to gunrunning. According to his file at the CIA, Merola was "a fast dealer with connections at all levels in many foreign countries." He was Cuban president Fulgencio Batista's personal pilot and flew the dictator into exile. An informer. Treacherous.

RABIN, WILLIAM (BILL), né Wolfe Rabinovitch (1907–1967). Musician, inventor, engineer, designer, promoter, serial entrepreneur, Wolfe is out for the main chance. You can see it in his swagger, in the finely tailored suits he wears, in his blonde, movie star–like wife. When he was a teenager in a Jewish immigrant family in a Canadian prairie town, Wolfe ran booze across the border during Prohibition. Rumors were that he had made a fortune and lost it four times over. Lavish and generous when he is on top, he imagines himself an industrialist like Howard Hughes. He is an outsider who dreams big, an underdog who defies society's expectations.

RABIN, GERTRUDE "TRUDY," née Rice (1907–1962). A streetwise blonde who models herself on actress Jean Harlow, leaves her family farm in Nebraska to make her way in the city. She has seen what happens to girls who hook up with wise guys, and while she might imitate Harlow's walk and speech, she is never going to be a gangster's moll. Although she plays tough, Wolfe can see the girl from the country; she reminds him of all the values of home and family. He offers her safety and security and treats her like a star. But underneath is a dreadful fear of what happens when you lose it all.

RABIN, LEON, né Leon Rabinovitch, aka Lee Cagney (1911–1969). Leon comes to Chicago with dreams of being a star, the drummer whose music is playing on the jukebox. With an uncanny resemblance, he poses as movie star James Cagney's brother. Girls adore him. He steps out from older brother Wolfe's shadow when he enlists in the U.S. Army at the start of World War II. When he returns a hero, he is happy to come home to his girl and a job in Wolfe's factory. A stalwart. Wolfe's voice of conscience and reason.

ROCKOLA, DAVID (1899–1991). Wolfe Rabin's archrival in the jukebox industry, Rockola also hails from a small town in Manitoba. The one-time blacksmith strikes it rich when he introduces the first jukebox with a twelve-disc changer, the self-named Rock-ola. He rules an operation that employs more than 3,000 workers and covers four square blocks in Chicago. He doubles his fortune when he converts his factory to making rifles in World War II. He will stop at nothing to crush the competition.

ROSDEN, GEORGE ERIC (1908–1993). A German businessman looking to make a score by introducing Americans to his banking contacts. Claims to have been an anti-Nazi and to have received immigration papers for services to the United States.

ROTHMAN, NORMAN "Roughhouse" or "Capper" (1907–1981). Husky, powerful, intimidating. With a rap sheet running from vagrancy to extortion, he is not to be crossed. Maintains one family with his Jewish wife Ethel in Miami and a second with Cuban dancer Olga Chaviano in Havana. Shares an immigrant Jewish heritage with Wolfe, has gained the trust of his Italian casino partners.

TOMLINSON, DOLLYE (born 1929). A willowy brunette who wins a beauty contest at seventeen, marries Kent Tomlinson at eighteen. Speaks in a sultry South Texas twang. Flies to Europe with Wolfe. Refuses to testify about the trip.

TOMLINSON, KENT (1914–1991). Pilot, dance instructor, Fuller Brush salesman, and inventor of the rubber chicken plucker finger. Married to a former beauty queen. Worships Wolfe, considers him his best friend.

Other family members: Beryl, Ruby, and Milton Rabinovitch.

With appearances by celebrity entertainers Sophie Tucker and Bing Crosby and baseball star Hank Greenburg.

Preface

On December 30, 1958, as revolutionary soldiers advanced on Havana, four men in fashionable suits wearing dark glasses crossed the tarmac at Miami airport and mounted the stairs to Pan Am flight 434. They were no ordinary tourists bound for New Year's revelry in the sin city of the Caribbean. Three of the men were kingpins of organized crime: Sam Mannarino, coin machine racketeer and head of the Pittsburgh family of La Cosa Nostra; Giuseppe "Pep" Cotroni, a narcotics trader, head of the Montreal Mafia; and Norman "Roughhouse" Rothman, nightclub and casino operator in Miami and Havana. The fourth man was reported only as a mysterious globetrotting financier. He was later identified as William "Wolfe" Rabin, my uncle.

How did my father's brother, raised in an immigrant Jewish family in a remote Canadian prairie town, become a jukebox tycoon, a crony of gangsters, and the mastermind behind an audacious and complex international money-laundering scheme? My investigation would reveal his world and a tale of jukeboxes, money laundering, and organized crime.

Wolfe was our family's deep dark secret, the black sheep whose exploits were mentioned only in fleeting whispers. I was intrigued by the myth and lore surrounding my uncle. Rumors were that he had made a fortune and lost it four times over. He invented the car radio. He was a wartime profiteer. He designed the first jet-age jukebox. He was an international bonds trader. Wolfe and his sexy wife Trudy were a glamorous couple.

There was only one photograph of Wolfe together with my father Milton, and I found it hidden under old documents at the bottom of a small strongbox. The black-and-white print of the two men counting money at a large wooden desk has the aura of a scene from the 1950s television crime drama *The Untouchables.*

I never met Wolfe and always wondered why. In a far-flung but close-knit family, I knew all my aunts and uncles except Wolfe and his wife Trudy. They were the only ones who didn't come to my bar mitzvah.

Despite my insatiable desire for information about Wolfe, I couldn't get much from my father. Was he protecting his brother or ashamed of him? He was secretive about Wolfe beyond his usual stoicism.

I determined to piece together Wolfe's story. It would be an investigation of a man whose accomplishments brought fame and power, only to end in obscurity, like *Citizen Kane.* I set out to find a "Rosebud," a clue to unlock the meaning of his life.

Thirty years later, after most of the players were gone, Milton recounted his version of the events and what drove his brother to extreme highs and lows. With a glass of scotch in one hand and a cigar crooked in the other, my father was an engaging storyteller.

He had amassed an eclectic collection of documents, mementos, items of intrinsic value like gold jewelry, and some objects whose significance was long forgotten. This odd array of things stored in files, shoeboxes, and cigar boxes yielded scraps of evidence from Wolfe's life—a World War II telegram, a 1937 invoice for an intercom system, schematics for radio patents, a 1924 poster for the family band, Wolfe Rabinovitch & the White Caps. Small pieces of a large puzzle. These fragments were intriguing but frustrating, as though the protagonist would determine how and when to reveal himself.

My years of research on the Web began to yield results, newspaper coverage of Wolfe's achievements in the music industry. Front-page headlines revealed more disturbing information about Wolfe's involvement with the Mob. A legal search produced a court judgment denying Wolfe's appeal of his conviction for possessing stolen bonds! On eBay, I found the original print of a 1962 photo of Wolfe and his lawyer outside a federal courtroom in Chicago. The lawyer was well known for defending Teamsters boss Jimmy Hoffa on racketeering charges. What was Wolfe's connection? Could this be related to the stolen bonds story?

With the assistance of researchers at the National Archives and Records Administration in Chicago and St. Louis, I obtained more than

1,000 pages of transcripts of trials in which Wolfe was a featured player. The transcripts had to be retrieved from the bowels of a federal storage facility in Skokie, Illinois. Nothing had been digitized, and even the current photocopies of the graying documents seemed impossibly musty.

I compiled a time line using newspaper reports, court documents, hotel registers, airline manifests, family photographs, and correspondence. In certain sequences, Wolfe's actions can be traced as in a daily diary. Some documents provide dialogue that can be quoted. And then there were frustrating gaps.

A series of scratchy seventy-eight-rpm discs called "recordios," made on a portable suitcase machine in the 1940s, yield impromptu recordings of Wolfe, brothers Leon and Milton, sisters Beryl and Ruby. They mailed these analog voice mails to their parents in Canada. The siblings are natural performers, their dialogue peppered with slang and quirky, idiosyncratic tough talk.

With a dog-eared business card of Wolfe's in hand, I went to a six-story industrial building on South Wabash Avenue in Chicago. Boarded up, windows smashed, abandoned and decaying, it had once been Wolfe's headquarters. I pictured a hub of industrial activity, hundreds of workers assembling jukeboxes, crating them, and loading them onto vans at the loading dock.

I explored locations found on letterheads, matchbooks, nightclub photographs, and the return address on home movie mailers. I found luxury hotel suites in Montreal, New York, and Zürich and a mid-century modern Florida condo in need of renovation. I looked for ghosts of my uncle, but he didn't appear.

I had reached a point where I had exhausted my research into my uncle's life when my work was inadvertently aided by an unexpected source. In 1992, Congress passed the John F. Kennedy Assassination Records Act in response to the furor over Oliver Stone's film *JFK*, which depicted the assassination as the work of senior CIA and Pentagon officials.[1] The act mandated that all files relating to the assassination be released within twenty-five years. With a deadline of October 2017, tens of thousands of files remained secret.

The FBI and CIA did not meet the deadline. Under pressure, more than 34,000 documents were released (or rereleased with fewer redactions) in seven batches in 2017 and 2018. I was incredulous. The name "William Rabin" aka "Wolfe Rabinovitch" appeared in dozens of files in investigations into money laundering, gunrunning, and other schemes. The files painted portraits of Wolfe's cohorts, friends, partners, adversaries. Was my father's brother somehow connected to the Kennedy assassination?

All the FBI agents who contributed to the reports are dead, impossible to interview for personal impressions and details. But their reports would enable me to locate the last living participant in Wolfe's escapades, his lover, the former beauty queen Dollye Tomlinson. Her story unfolds in the pages ahead.

What would my father have said if he had known what I would expose about his brother's actions and character? Although I never met my uncle, he left me something incredible: his story.

Much of my work in writing this book has been to perceive the relationships of people and events that were intended to remain secret. Faced with connecting the dots in the factual narrative, I have imagined some scenes and what might have been said. Although I never met Wolfe, I have come to know him. It's in the family DNA.

Figure b.1. Wolfe on the $1,000 bill. The $1,000 bill was the preferred unit of currency for money laundering operations. COLLAGE BY THE AUTHOR.

Introduction

WHEN I STARTED RESEARCHING THIS BOOK, I CAME ACROSS HEADLINES in the entertainment journal *Billboard* about the lawsuit over patents between Wolfe Rabin and the jukebox pioneer David Rockola. That led me to dig into the untold history of the jukebox and the competition to continually improve the mechanics and design of the coin-operated music machines. At this point, my view was that the story was about technology, invention, and entrepreneurship in twentieth-century America. I saw my uncle as the gifted son of immigrants striving for the American dream. He earned a university degree; he had an intuition for electronics; he passed the exam for a pilot's license.

When Wolfe Rabin built the Maestro with its thirty-disc selection after World War II, it was a sensational breakthrough, as was his use of jet-age plastics and aluminum replacing the traditional wooden cabinets. He designed and manufactured a jukebox that became an icon of popular culture, only to get entangled in a vicious patent war that went all the way to the Supreme Court. This is the end of the first story arc, sowing the seeds of an even larger and more dangerous narrative.

Wolfe got out of the coin machine business, a hotbed of Mob activity, in 1949. The next year, the Kefauver investigation into organized crime in interstate commerce, the first televised Senate hearings, captured the public interest.

With his jukebox empire in ruins, Wolfe had a new vision: high fidelity in the American home. A serial entrepreneur in an era when most Americans seek job security, Wolfe's vision was a success. His new venture, Continental Radio Corporation, rode the crest of 1950s consumerism. He was back in *Billboard*.

Wolfe bought a house in Highland Park, a prestigious Chicago suburb. Then the trail of documentation went cold. And something went terribly wrong. Wolfe bottomed out. He sold the house. He borrowed money from his brother Leon.

At exactly the moment when the second narrative arc in Wolfe's story began, a new Senate inquiry into labor racketeering, led by committee counsel Robert F. Kennedy, started making headlines. Wolfe's cronies from the coin machine industry were subpoenaed to testify.

Wolfe surfaced in Miami in 1958. He would be drawn into a venture with high stakes. Up against powerful forces, Wolfe was caught between the Mob and the feds at the nexus of an epic caper that rivals the movie *Ocean's 11*. A diverse crew pulled off a complex plot involving Canadian bonds, Swiss banks, and Cuban casinos—what international law enforcement called the biggest bank robbery in the world and the largest money-laundering scheme in history—and then it came undone. Fidel Castro's communists took power in Cuba and closed the casinos. But Wolfe and his Mob associates would not go on trial until 1962.

Americans have always been attracted to the stories of outlaws, of antiheroes who challenge the system, who pull off feats that most of us would never have the nerve to perform. My uncle had the charm to pull off a con and the balls to go for the big score. But he was undermined by his own hubris. This arc reveals another dimension of the immigrant experience: Wolfe was an outsider—to the Mafia, to law enforcement, and even to some in his family.

My grandfather had journeyed across half the planet to find freedom. Born with that freedom, Wolfe Rabin went in search of the American dream.

CHAPTER ONE

Origins

LITTLE *SHTETL* ON THE PRAIRIE
Morden, Manitoba

LIKE HIS CONTEMPORARY HOWARD HUGHES, WOLFE WAS A SELF-taught designer, pilot, and inventor. From small-town origins, he aimed for the big stage.

On a frigid January night in 1907, Wolfe was born in the home of Russian Jewish immigrants who had pioneered in the Canadian farming community of Morden on the remote Manitoba plains. My grandfather's emigration is our family's version of *Fiddler on the Roof*.

In 1889, my namesake ancestor David Rabinovitch, twenty-three, married with two daughters, fled Cossacks attacking Jews in a *shtetl*[1] outside Kiev. He walked across Europe, finding shelter in Jewish villages. The stocky, determined young man made his way to Danzig,[2] where he just missed a ship bound for New York. In a twist of fate, he boarded a ship embarking for Canada, his passage paid by Baron de Hirsch, an Austrian philanthropist who financed resettlement of Jews fleeing persecution.[3]

On arrival in Halifax, David encountered a recruiter offering passage to the west in return for labor on the harvest. He wanted to know if there was land for sale on this far-off frontier. "For as far as the eye can see," came the response. Unlike the restricted life in the old country, in Canada, a Jew could even buy land. He rode the recently completed Canadian Pacific railroad across half the continent, arriving in southern Manitoba, which reminded him of the steppes of Ukraine.

After harvesting wheat to pay off his indebtedness, the young man settled in the pioneer town of Morden, population 1,000. He had learned the grain trade in Russia and soon began brokering crops for farmers, enabling them to survive the winter by making loans against a share of the future crop. He was, in effect, a commodities options trader.

As more immigrants came to the area, David saw an opportunity and opened a general store. He grew popular for selling alcoholic patent medicines in the dry town, earning the nickname "Doc."

Invigorated by the air of freedom, Doc worked and saved for six years to bring his wife Leah and two daughters from the old country. At last, he eagerly journeyed to greet them at the CPR station in Winnipeg. But when the reunited family returned by train to Morden, a raging fire had consumed Doc's store. The people of the town took up a collection to help their industrious neighbor rebuild. Then a deeper tragedy struck. Leah died of typhoid fever. Left alone with his two young girls, Doc needed a wife.

Word got around the Jewish community in the province of Manitoba. A wife would be arranged. The *shochet*[4] in Winnipeg had a younger sister in New York.

Like thousands of young immigrant women in the 1890s, Sonia Kluner sewed piecework in a sweatshop on the Lower East Side of Manhattan. She was constantly in trouble for organizing, instigating, and championing to improve the working conditions. Her brother's summons to Canada to marry a man she had never met would be her escape from exploitation. How could she ask for greater fortune? Her brother would provide her dowry.

Imagine the trepidation the willowy seventeen-year-old must have felt as she stepped down from the train at the CPR station in Winnipeg, a booming city in the middle of the prairie at the turn of the twentieth century. She had spent the three-day journey from New York wondering about the man to whom she was betrothed. In their wedding photo (1900), Doc and Sonia make an unusual couple, the tall teenage bride with her stocky husband, five inches shorter and thirteen years her senior.

From all accounts, they found a deep love together, raising seven children. Doc and Sonia instilled in their offspring a strong work ethic, family loyalty, and an appreciation of the wondrous opportunity in North America.

Wolfe was in the middle of a rambunctious brood of seven (plus two older half sisters from Doc's first marriage), each with their own dramas and triumphs. Anne, Wolfe's eldest sister, went to nursing school, married a doctor, and became a doyenne of culture in Saskatchewan. Archie, his elder brother, denied entry to medical schools by the unwritten quotas for Jews, went to Toronto to study dentistry. Sister Ruby left for New York, where she enjoyed success as a writer and was invited to join the literati at the Algonquin Round Table.

Wolfe was the fourth child, athletic, popular, and smart. My father Milton was two years younger, tall, broad-shouldered, good-natured, the son who stayed home to mind the store and look after his parents. Two years after Milton came Leon, the fourth Rabinovitch brother. Stocky, blonde, he grew up with a remarkable resemblance to movie tough guy Jimmy Cagney. The youngest sibling had her own dreams of stardom. Beryl, the third sister, won a Bette Davis look-alike contest at nineteen and was a heartbreaker herself. But all agreed that Wolfe was a man of destiny, the one who would break boundaries, whose exploits would capture the imagination.[5]

Morden, 1922

Two boys, Wolfe, fifteen, and his youngest brother Leon, eleven, pick their way over the tracks and rails in the CPR's Morden freight yard, sharing a cigarette. Long trains of boxcars stand motionless on the track, with names stenciled on their sides: Canadian Pacific, Soo Line, Great Northern. The boys stare at the cars with wide-eyed longing.

> Wolfe: I'm going to get on one of these trains and it's going to take me to Chicago.
> Leon: Me? I want to go to California. See the Specific Ocean.
> Wolfe: You mean Pacific Ocean.

The boys laugh. Wolfe stubs out his cigarette.

Sauntering along the track, Wolfe notices a freight car, unlocked. He pulls himself up, peers inside through a crack in the door. He sees stacks of cardboard boxes. He calls to Leon. "C'mon."

In the dimly lit car, the boys open a box. It's full of safety razors and blue blades. They grab handfuls of razors and blades, stuffing them into their pockets.

Outside along the track, a watchman patrols the rail yard. He peers under trains, looking for hoboes. He notices the open door to the freight car. He points his lantern into the car. The boys crouch behind a stack of boxes.

The watchman calls. "Come on out of there!"

Wolfe motions to Leon. The boys make a break for it, leaping out the door past the watchman. Lantern swaying, he chases after them.

The boys round a corner into an alley, racing to the fence at the end of it. Wolfe jumps and pulls himself up, razors and blades spilling out of his pockets. Leon reaches the fence as the watchman catches up.

Straddling the top of the fence, Wolfe looks back. "C'mon, Leon, jump." He drops to the other side.

Leon jumps, catches the top, and is just drawing himself up when the watchman's hands seize his legs and pull him down.

The watchman recognizes Leon, who looks ashamed. "Which one of your brothers got away?" Leon stays silent.

The watchman tells Leon he is going to take him to old Doc Rabinovitch. Leon can explain himself to his father.[6]

The radio crackles in the attic of the old three-story Victorian house. Wearing a headset, young Wolfe tunes the crystal to signals from far-off stations. He keeps a log, a hobby known as DXing. He is enchanted by the music on stations like WGN Chicago.

Early radio brought the Jazz Age to the town, and most of the family was musically inclined. Wolfe plays sax and cornet and starts a dance band with brother Leon on drums and sister Ruby, who plays piano to accompany silent films at the town's movie house, on piano. Wolfe Rabinovitch & the White Caps play dance halls in small-town Manitoba and North Dakota. My father Milton, the big fellow, sells tickets and acts as bouncer when the country crowd turns rowdy.

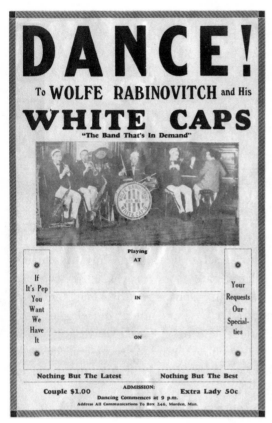

Figure 1.1. Poster for Wolfe Rabinovitch and the White Caps, circa 1924. Wolfe plays cornet, frame left, brother Leon on drums, sister Ruby on piano. COPYRIGHT THE AUTHOR.

Wolfe went to Winnipeg to study pharmacy at age seventeen. Home from university on weekends, he worked in the town drugstore, which sold liquor under the counter. With bootleg liquor supplied by the Bronfman brothers Charles and Sam, immigrant Jewish cohorts of Wolfe's father Doc, the Morden pharmacy was one of a string of outlets strategically located along the border with the United States to capitalize on a trade of thirsty Americans escaping Prohibition.

The Volstead Act, a constitutional amendment prohibiting the production, import, transport, and sale of liquor, came into force in the United States in 1920. Conversely, prohibition had ended in Canada after World War I. Under Canadian law, selling liquor for export was legal. The enterprising Bronfmans saw the opportunity to go legitimate and bought a royal charter to import British liquor to Canada. But the big money—and the risk—lay in exporting this high-quality booze to the United States. Prohibition would result in the biggest outlaw culture of all time in America. The cities came under the control of a growing underworld of racketeers who gained power through the illegal liquor trade and the fortunes it promised. These were the Bronfmans' American customers and the origin of the Seagram liquor fortune.

Wolfe quickly became a trusted driver for the Bronfmans. In his father's powerful McLaughlin-Buick, he navigated the deep coulee south of town where there are still no border inspection stations into North Dakota. Lights out under the moonlight, laden with crates of whiskey, the big car made the grade with Wolfe at the wheel on frequent runs to the United States. My father told me that one morning after Wolfe had the car out, it came back with a bullet hole in the fender.

Secret fraternities played a significant role in society in that era. The Masonic Order, with no restrictions on color or creed, appealed to young Jewish men. Joining provided access to a worldwide network of trustworthy connections.

Following his father and two of his brothers, Wolfe joined the local Masonic lodge. In the ritual of initiation into the ancient brotherhood, he swore a solemn oath to never reveal the secrets of Masonry, "under no less a penalty than having my throat cut across, my tongue torn out, or the more effective punishment of being branded as a willfully perjured individual, void of all moral worth, unfit to be received into the society of men who prize honor and virtue."[7]

It is the first of several oaths Wolfe will take along his journey, one vow that he will never break.

How proud Doc and Sonia must have been when Wolfe was awarded his degree, the fourth of their offspring to graduate from university. A photo behind the pharmacy counter shows a nattily dressed young man with a great mop of hair and the familial widow's peak. But a job mixing potions and dispensing prescriptions is not the career he has in mind. He yearns for the bright lights and big city, determined to go to Chicago to seek his fortune.

Horse-drawn wagons and tin lizzies deliver passengers and deposit cargo at the Morden railway station, a classic CPR building from 1905. Looking sharp in a new wool suit, Wolfe leaves the ticket window for the boardwalk bustling with people and carts. He looks across the street to his father's emporium—"D. Rabinovitch, General Merchant," lettered on the windows. Doc emerges through the barrels of grain, sugar, apples, and coal on the boardwalk, scans the platform across the street, raises his cane, and waves it at Wolfe. Through hard work and grit, his immigrant father

Figure 1.2. Wolfe climbs a telephone pole, circa 1929. Stunts were popular in the Roaring Twenties. COPYRIGHT THE ESTATE OF NICK YUDELL, USED BY PERMISSION.

has made a success in the new land. But clerking in the family store is not in Wolfe's future.

The conductor calls, "All aboard!" Valise in hand, Wolfe steps up to the passenger car. His tearful mother Sonia hugs him and presses a dollar into his hand—traveling *tzeda-kah*[8] so that he will never be broke. He promises to write to her.

Steam belches from the locomotive as it gathers speed. Wolfe appears in a window, watching the prairies rush by, dreaming of music, girls, and striking it rich in Chicago.

Chicago, 1928

Justus P. Seeburg, a mechanically gifted Swedish immigrant, makes a fortune building and marketing the "Orchestrion"—a coin-operated mechanically played piano equipped with various other instruments, including violins, mandolin, flute, snare drum, cymbal, triangle, and other percussion effects. With changing tastes in music and the advent of radio in the mid-1920s, locations wanted a machine that could play records with vocals. In 1928, Seeburg creates the Audiophone, a coin-operated music machine with eight turntables that rotate on a Ferris-wheel mechanism. Weighing more than five hundred pounds, it is the ancestor of the jukebox phenomenon that will explode ten years later.

NEMESIS
Chicago, October 1929

Wolfe arrives in Chicago looking for the main chance. At the height of Prohibition, Al Capone's gang rules the Windy City. And another young man from Manitoba gains notoriety as the "Crown Prince of the Slots."

Like Wolfe Rabinovitch, David Rockola hails from a small town in rural Manitoba.[9] Like Wolfe, he had migrated to Chicago to seek his fortune ten years earlier. He will become Wolfe's bitter rival.

Rockola came from a hardscrabble background. Born in 1897, the child of Russian immigrants, he grew up apprenticed to his father, a blacksmith. His parents separated, and his mother died when he was fourteen. Young David went to work as a bellhop at a hotel in Saskatoon, staying up late to work on correspondence courses that he never completed.

Still a teenager, he moved to the Hotel Laurel in Medicine Hat, Alberta, where he ran the cigar counter. Later in life, Rockola would recount a story, perhaps apocryphal, about a salesman who came in to promote a "trade stimulator"—a type of coin-operated gumball machine that dispensed prizes, like vouchers for items in the shop.[10] His customers fed coins into the novelty. Rockola's fascination with coin-operated machines would become his driving force.

Baby-faced but street smart, Rockola arrived in Chicago at the beginning of the Roaring Twenties. He found work as a mechanic for slot machine companies. Vending machines, gumballs, games of chance, he learned the mechanisms, making notes for improvements.

By 1927, at age 30, he is ready to gamble on himself. With his young wife and a few assistants, he starts the Rockola Scale Company, manufacturing penny scales, which are in demand for arcades and drugstores. He develops a sideline that will become the real moneymaker—retrofitting illegal devices to slot machines to give immediate payouts.

The slots appealed to the gambling instinct in almost everyone. Who doesn't want to make money by merely pulling a handle? Unscrupulous operators saw the opportunities to rig the games, shortchange the payouts, and skim the untraceable profits to avoid taxes.[11] The slots presented issues of morality to some, evidence of growing criminal activity to others.

The State of Illinois operated under a ruling that slot machines that did not give cash payouts (but rather tokens or vouchers that could be redeemed for cash) were legal. Several states had this rule to make certain that jackpot payouts were as displayed. After all, it wasn't unknown for operators to short the winnings.[12] By 1928, "so many machines were placed in operation that truant officers were compelled to demand that the police remove the machines from the vicinity of school buildings where school children frequently gambled on the machines."[13]

As his business developed, Rockola acquired more than one hundred slot machines. He went to Jimmy "High Pockets" O'Brien, kingpin of the South Side slot syndicate. "High Pockets" got his moniker from his extreme height. Rockola proposed a deal.

"He told me that if I wanted to pay him 75 percent of the receipts I could go ahead and install machines in different districts . . . and for that 75 percent he would take care of the protection of the machines, see that the local police would not interfere, and also the police downtown," Rockola told an investigator.[14]

In 1928, Chicago elected a reform administration charged with cleaning up corruption, and a new state's attorney was appointed to lead the effort. The slot machine syndicates became the target of the investigation.

The commission investigated every aspect of the slot business, questioning manufacturers, owners, distributors, and players. The state's attorney presented the case to a grand jury. Based on the testimony of David Rockola and others, the state filed bribery and corruption of public morals charges against the South Side slot syndicate.[15] Indictments were issued to Jimmy "High Pockets" O'Brien, six police captains, prominent politicians, and city officials.

When the case finally comes to trial in 1929, Rockola agrees to testify in return for a grant of immunity. He will be the star witness. But when he is called to the stand, Rockola pleads the Fifth Amendment, claiming that testifying may cause him to incriminate himself. It's an extraordinary move, as he has already been granted immunity from prosecution.

The judge considers bringing conspiracy charges against him. He finds Rockola in contempt of court and sentences him to six months in Cook County Jail.

Without Rockola's testimony, the state's case collapses.

From his cell, Rockola sends word to Jimmy High Pockets: "I never ratted out nobody."

Wolfe scans the papers at a newsstand. The headlines are all about the Crown Prince of the Slots. Welcome to Chicago.

BRIGHT LIGHTS, BIG CITY

When Wolfe descends the train at Chicago's Union Station, he is immediately struck at the presence of so many African Americans: the porter who grabs his valise, the row of shoeshine men, the news vendor hawking his papers—"Tribune Final! Rockola Goes to Jail! Tribune Final!"

There were no Black people in Morden, maybe even none in the whole province of Manitoba, Wolfe mused. But he had listened to Black musicians on the radio—Louis Armstrong, Fats Waller, Duke Ellington—and he was eager to hear his idols play in the speakeasies and blind pigs.

A friendly Black hotel doorman gives him directions. Wolfe gets a room in a rooming house for a dollar a night. He lathers up, shaves with a straight-edge razor. Looking in the mirror, he's pleased with the results. Slaps on after-shave, smooths his hair back, pops a Sen-Sen in his mouth, cracks it open. Fastens his tie, shrugs into his suit coat. Ready for his first night in Chicago. On the way out the door, grabs his cornet case.

He turns down an alley, looking for an address. He approaches a green door, raps his knuckles on it. A peephole slides open; a heavy guy demands to know who sent him. Wolfe raises his cornet case. He's a musician.

The tough guy relaxes, lets him inside. He points Wolfe down a long corridor with plumbing pipes and electrical circuits. "Go through the tunnel," he directs.

Wolfe emerges from the end of the tunnel through a vault-like door into a large club filled with dozens of people drinking and dancing to jazz from a Black combo. He is assaulted by the din of music, clinking glasses, voices shouting to be heard. Prohibition had resulted in an entirely new, often literally underground, illegal drinking establishment. Gone were the men-only saloons and bars of pre-1920 America. Since their replacements could only be whispered about, they became known as speakeasies. There are an estimated three thousand speakeasies in Chicago in 1929.

Wolfe approaches the stage, takes his cornet from its case. The band-leader motions for him to join. He purses his lips, picks up the tune. The musicians nod with approval. When it's Wolfe's turn, he cuts loose with a cool solo and is rewarded with applause from the crowd.

He jumps down from the stage into the teeming dance floor. A slender redhead in a short sequined dress, arms and shoulders bare, shimmies up to him. She's a Jazz Age woman, a flapper, women who go to the speaks unescorted, who drink and smoke and dance the hoochie-coo.

"You're good on that horn!" she beckons him. "Wanna dance?"

They dance the Charleston, the jitterbug, the foxtrot. It's hot and sweaty and smoky. They drink. And drink. And drink.

When Wolfe wakes up, he's uncertain where he is or how he got there. He finds himself on a mattress on the floor, and the red-haired flapper is leaning over him, staring intently.

"Hey wolf-man! I thought you'd never wake up."

Embarrassed, he asks her name. She introduces herself. Stella Atkins[16] from Chicago, and she is going to be an artist.

He looks around, sees works in progress on various easels. Paint-spattered walls. Canvases stacked on the floor. Stella makes coffee on a hotplate. He's never met a woman like her before. She's nothing like the prim and proper country girls in Morden or the put-a-ring-on-my-finger Jewish girls in Winnipeg.

In the weeks that follow, they cruise the speakeasies, drinking and dancing every night. They are smitten with each other. She introduces him to her friends, an unconventional group of painters, actors, and writers. They go to the movies, where the conversion from silent film to "talkies" is filling the movie palaces. Stella takes him to foreign films, like *L'age d'or*, directed by the Spanish surrealist Luis Bunuel, but Wolfe can't make heads or tails out of it.

Both are captured by the charisma of Marlene Dietrich as a cabaret singer who wraps an aging professor around her little finger in *The Blue Angel*. Wolfe has no problem following the dialogue in German; it's kind of like the Yiddish his parents spoke at home.

He convinces her to see an American film, a comedy with the Marx Brothers. He waits for her under the marquee for *Animal Crackers*. When Stella arrives, she is distraught.

"I'm late." She stops.

Wolfe checks his watch. "Ten minutes to showtime. No problem."

That's not what she means.

Beat.

She's pregnant.

He reddens, thunderstruck. Long silence.

Wolfe: We could get married. Ma would never talk to me again. She would say that I'm dead.

Stella: I don't want to get married. You're a great guy, but—

Wolfe: I'll find a way to take care of it.

Stella: No. Not that. I'm going to have the baby.

This is a lot to take in. All the consequences. She takes him by the arm.

Stella: Just because I'm having a baby doesn't mean we can't go to the movies, does it?

Chicago, July 9, 1930

Wolfe is in his room at the boardinghouse, at the desk, staring at a sheet of foolscap. He takes out a fountain pen, dips the nib in the inkwell, and begins writing. His penmanship has a classic flourish.

Dear Stella,

Congratulations on the birth of our baby girl. I regret that I will never see her, that she will never know me, but this is as you requested, and I will respect your wishes. It is for the best. If only things were different.

I am enclosing some $$$ to help with the baby.

Love,

Wolfe

He blows on the paper to dry the ink, folds the letter, and tucks it into an envelope. He takes a ten-dollar bill from his wallet, slips it in with the letter.

He has a pang of regret for what might have been. How could he be a father, now? He is only twenty-three, and he hasn't got the means or the maturity. This baby will be his deepest secret. No one will ever know of her existence.

Wolfe gets a job in a radio repair shop. His boyhood hobby, tinkering with his crystal sets, becomes his ticket to success. Using the latest vacuum tubes, he designs a radio small enough that it can be installed in an automobile and powered by the car's battery.

The car radio had been a dream as radio stations and a network of highways spread across America in the 1920s. Technology was primitive, requiring large batteries, a cabinet full of vacuum tubes, and an antenna the size of the roof. By the early 1930s, Motorola introduced a downsized radio with improved reception. Everyone who bought a car wanted one. Many were concerned that playing the radio in the car was dangerous, and some jurisdictions passed "distracted driving" laws.

Wolfe sees the opportunity. He mounts a display of his radio at the 1933 Century of Progress Exposition, and the response is encouraging. His brother Milton drives down from Canada to see the world's fair, and Wolfe installs a radio in Milt's Desoto sedan.[17]

A few aisles away, David Rockola's booth is crowded with fairgoers playing Jigsaw, an exciting new pinball machine, state of the art in interactive gaming for 1933. The Crown Prince of the Slots had done time for contempt in the Chicago coin machine trials, but on appeal, the verdict was vacated, and in 1932, Rockola asked for and received executive clemency from the state.[18] He is back in business.

Even in the depths of the Great Depression, people still dig into their pockets for a penny or a nickel for the entertainment that pinball machines provide. Rockola turns to designing and manufacturing coin-operated games. Jigsaw—which gives the player ten balls for five cents—will be wildly successful and sell more than 70,000 units.

Encouraged by the response to his own exhibit, Wolfe incorporates a company to manufacture radios. He sends for his brother Leon, four years younger, who comes to Chicago to work for Wolfe. Still dreaming of a career as a drummer in a big band, he lives in a rooming house where he shuts himself in the closet to practice drumming. Leon changes his name, adopting the stage name Lee Cagney at the suggestion of an agent who sees the resemblance and promotes him as movie star James Cagney's brother.

Cruising Michigan Avenue in Wolfe's roadster, Leon grips the wheel. Adjusting the car radio, Wolfe's head turns at the sight of a platinum blonde, high heels clicking on the sidewalk. Leon whistles.

Wolfe: She's got class. Pull over.

Leon turns the car to the curb. Wolfe opens the door, steps out in front of the young woman.

Wolfe: Going south?
Trudy: I'm not accustomed to riding with strangers.
Wolfe: We're not going to be strangers.
Trudy: I don't date wise guys.

A streetwise young woman who styles herself after movie star Jean Harlow, Gertrude Rice left her family farm in Iowa to make her way in the city. She has seen what happens to girls who hook up with wise guys, and while she might imitate Harlow's walk and speech, she is never going to be a gangster's moll.

Wolfe: C'mon. My driver will take us.

He is handsome, cocky, charming. She purses her lips, intrigued. She slides onto the seat between Wolfe and his cute blonde brother at the wheel. They drive along Lakeshore Blvd, wind blowing off Lake Michigan.

The roadster stops at her corner. Wolfe opens the door, gallantly helps Trudy to the street.

Wolfe: What's your name?
Trudy: It's Gertrude. You can call me Trudy.
Wolfe: Can I see you later?
Trudy: Sure, you can give me a call sometime.

She pencils a number on a scrap of paper.

Wolfe: I mean later today![19]

Although she plays tough, Wolfe can see past the veneer. She is a straight talker who can hold her own.

Chicago has become Wolfe Rabin's city; he knows it like the back of his hand, the hotels and ballrooms, the back alleys and blind pigs, the Ritz-Carlton and the Turkish *shvitz*. He has a nodding acquaintance with the people who are the inner gears of the metropolis—the news vendor on the corner, the bellman at the hotel gate, the cabbies in their Checkers, the barbers and bookies and bartenders and the maître d's who get you a prime table. Wolfe seduces Trudy with his charm, big ideas—and jewelry.

While millions of Americans haunt breadlines, manufacturing radios is profitable during the Depression, and Wolfe reaps the rewards. He files patent applications for television, the medium of the future. He changes his name to William Rabin, more modern, and takes the oath to become an American citizen. With Leon as his best man, he marries Trudy at City Hall. No Jewish wedding for Wolfe. His family will just have to accept her.

CHAPTER TWO

Pay to Play

A BRIEF HISTORY OF THE JUKEBOX INDUSTRY SETS THE STAGE FOR
Wolfe Rabin's rise as a coin machine tycoon.

When President Ronald Reagan proclaimed National Jukebox Week
in 1988, he called the jukebox "a symbol of good, clean fun, and a
treasury of memories for listeners of every generation. For a century now,
the jukebox has been a fixture of popular culture in our land."[1]

Behind the impact of jukeboxes on American culture lies a story of
technology and crime. The pay-for-play music machine is born in San
Francisco in November 1889 when Louis Glass introduces his "put-a-
nickel-in-the-slot phonograph" in a Gay Nineties gin joint. Glass had
developed a passion for the new field of electronics while working as
a telegraph operator for Western Union. Following Thomas Edison's
invention of the phonograph, Glass incorporated the Pacific Phonograph
Company and attached a coin-operated device to monetize the machine.
Powered by a twenty-five-pound battery in a large wooden cabinet, his
unit plays one mechanical cylinder while four people at a time hold
listening tubes to their ears. A month later, Glass files a patent appli-
cation for a "coin activated attachment for phonographs." Glass later
claims that his machine took in $1,000 in six months—a huge number of
five-cent coins. But the machine wasn't practical to produce and
distribute, and the concept languished. The term "jukebox" will not come
into use until nearly fifty years later. In keeping with the theme of invention and investigation, Glass will later be convicted of bribery in a plot to
create a monopoly on telephone service in San Francisco.[2]

Coin-operated products in those years, according to jukebox pioneer David Rockola, included player pianos, phonographs, banjos, xylophones, other mechanized musical instruments, and even talking pictures. All of those coin-operated machines employed discs with music recorded on them. The coin-operated piano used perforated rolls, although some had discs. The coin-operated phonographs first played cylinders and later recorded discs. At that time, many of those coin-operated phonographs were equipped with earphones. But by 1894, the loudspeaker horn had come into popular use, and the enjoyment of jukebox music was no longer limited to one person at a time.[3]

With the end of Prohibition in 1932, thousands of newly legal taverns needed a music machine to provide entertainment, cheaper than paying musicians.

"Prohibition had been repealed and bars were opening up all over. People needed cheap entertainment, and I got to thinking about music," Rockola later recalled.[4]

Coin-operated player pianos provided music in some bars but were seen as old-fashioned. The first jukeboxes offered only one disc, and each seventy-eight-rpm record played only one song. In their large wood cabinets, early jukeboxes were an expensive novelty.

The competition to invent a coin-operated multidisc phonograph began. With improved electronics and mechanics, by the mid-1930s, the automatic music machines developed the capacity to play up to ten records. Coin-operated phonographs become a phenomenon. The WurliTzer, Seeburg, and Rock-ola companies dominate the industry.

With exploding sales, jukebox production increases tenfold. Even at the nadir of the Depression, anyone could afford a nickel for a song.

Because they are in constant use, jukeboxes require frequent servicing to change the record lineup and replace worn-out needles and records. Out-of-work bootleggers seize the opportunity. A system of territorial enforcement is established.

Jukebox manufacturers sell their machines only to distributors, never directly to location owners. The distributors sell to operators who place the boxes, service them, and run the routes to collect the cash from the machines. Distributors often keep the best routes for themselves through affiliated companies.

Production increases from 25,000 in 1934 to 400,000 in 1940. The *New York Times*, in the feature "The Ubiquitous Juke Box," predicts "it will be one of the nation's larger industries—like automobiles or the movies."[5] The mint can't produce enough nickels to feed the machines.[6]

"Juke"—translated as rowdy or wicked—came from the Gullahs, a group of African American descendants of slaves who spoke a form of Creole in the southeastern United States.[7] The industry discourages the term "jukebox," conjuring images of Black shanties on cotton plantations. "The jooks [*sic*] are an escape from this way of life," the *Saturday Evening Post* notes in a 1941 feature.[8]

And my Mama said, Do you know what goes on in a juke house? Boy don't you know there's gambling, And a whole lotta drinking, And a lotta hot women. And I don't want no boy of mine in a juke house.
—Blind Mississippi Morris and Brad Webb[9]

Despite the racism that extends throughout the jukebox industry, from the music selection to older models kept in service at the juke joints, the term sticks as the boxes pervade.

Lovely to look at but dangerous to love. She's a good girl for guys to leave alone. —Taglines for Juke Girl *(1942)*[10]

The music machines are in the mainstream of American culture with the 1942 release of the B-movie *Juke Girl* starring Ann Sheridan as a dime-a-dance girl who hooks up with Ronald Reagan, a migrant worker from the Kansas cornfields who starts a one-man crusade against the local big-shot packer. Despite the star appeal, *New York Times* critic Bosley Crowther dismisses the film. "The whole smacks too much of the synthetic. It's like a tune that comes out of a juke box."[11]

WAR

Chicago, December 31, 1941

The poster at the Trianon Ballroom features the Lee Cagney Band. Leon backs a big band with a horn section and a singer with a lusty voice.

Although the crowd is drinking and dancing, this New Year's is fraught with foreboding. Pearl Harbor had been attacked by Japan three weeks earlier. America is going to war. The performance at the Trianon will be Leon's last.

Leon takes the opportunity to step out from Wolfe's shadow. Holding hands with his girl Val, he informs Wolfe and Trudy that he has enlisted in the U.S. Army. Val, a warmhearted brunette with big brown eyes, swears she'll wait for him.

With his knowledge of electronics, Sergeant Leon Rabinovitch is assigned to a signals unit. As he departs Union Station on a troop train, Wolfe cautions him to watch his back. Who is going to watch yours? The words form in Leon's mind but remain unspoken. Instead, he asks Wolfe to keep an eye out for his gal Val.

Chicago, 1942

America is in a catch-up mode. The War Department throws millions of dollars at contractors for desperately needed materiel, an extraordinary opportunity for an entrepreneur with production capability. Wolfe converts the radio factory to manufacturing communications systems for the armed forces. With men drafted into the services, he staffs up with the disabled, women, and African Americans. He proudly displays a patriotic billboard with a bald eagle and a shield that reads "Arsenal of Democracy."

Trudy sashays through the factory floor at Rabin Industries, hot legs in hard-to-get nylons. Wolf whistles pierce the din. Good-natured, she waves. Good for morale. She ascends stairs to the catwalk to Wolfe's office above.

Tie loosened, vest open, shirt sleeves rolled up, Wolfe toils round the clock, and his factory works overtime producing radios, receivers, and intercoms contracted for the army and air force. He personally tests each unit. He is not one of those wartime profiteers who cut corners to line their pockets. Not when his brother's life and the lives of American men depend on his radios.

The War Production Board had ordered that the manufacture of non-essential items like coin machines and jukeboxes cease and that factories be converted to meet the war needs. David Rockola's company converted to making M1 rifles. A lightweight semiautomatic shoulder arm that fired a

.30-caliber cartridge, the M1 became the most popular rifle for the U.S. Army. Since Rock-ola was well versed in fabricating wooden cabinets for its jukeboxes, the company made its own carbine stocks and hand guards.[12] Over the war years, Army Ordnance contracted with Rock-ola for 228,000 M1 rifles worth $42 million.

Art Institute of Chicago, March 12, 1942

Wolfe, in tuxedo, and Trudy, in a mink stole, mingle with the crowd at the Art Institute of Chicago—opening night for a showcase of area artists. Trudy turns up her nose at the upper-crust clientele. "Since when are you interested in art?" she demands of Wolfe.

"I could be a patron of the arts," he replies. "Good for business."

Draws on his cigar. He likes the sound of that. Patron of the arts.

They make their way through the exhibition, commenting on the paintings. Wolfe stops by one titled "My Studio" by Stella Lamperti. He does a double take. He recognizes Stella's studio from a dozen years earlier when he had first arrived in Chicago.

And then he sees her—Stella—in the midst of a group of people, laughing, drinking cocktails. One man is very attentive, her husband Michael Lamperti, an attorney with a reputation for integrity. Michael points toward Stella's painting, motions the group in Wolfe's direction.

Wolfe came here looking for something, but he is not prepared for this moment.

He takes Trudy by the arm, hustles her away.

Stella's reputation in the Chicago arts community grows. A few months later, with funding from her husband, she opens the Studio of Ceramic Arts. The *Chicago Tribune* reports that "Mrs. Lamperti recently spent a year in Mexico painting and learning pottery making. The new studio is a development of her Mexican experience."[13]

Army Base, Classified, South Pacific, 1944

In the radio shack on a remote island in the South Pacific, Leon adjusts his headset. He tunes out the propaganda of Tokyo Rose, sweeps the dial for enemy signals. The radio crackles with static. With a stubby pencil, Leon writes to his family on onionskins.[14]

"I can't find the words, Mother and Milton to tell you how grateful I am for going to see Val and I want to thank you Ma for the gift you gave her."

The letter reveals a rift between Leon's fiancée Val, who is working as a saleswoman at Marshall Fields department store, and Wolfe's glamorous wife Trudy. Is it because Val is a good Jewish girl with approval from Wolfe's mother, something Trudy can never earn?

"I can't say I'm very pleased with Trudy's actions regarding Val," Leon continues. "I don't know what she has against her. We've never asked her for anything and in fact have gone out of our way to be nice to her, so whatever it is that causes her to act like a child is beyond me."

The letter passes the censors and reaches Morden, Manitoba, six weeks later. In the kitchen of the big Victorian, warmed by a wood-burning stove, Sonia reads her son Leon's missive. A concerned look crosses her face. Worry, a mother's worry.

"*Mechel.*" She calls Milton by his Yiddish name. "That *shiksa*. Wolfe's movie star. She's making trouble between the boys."

VJ Day, August 8, 1945

The family rejoices at the victory over Japan and the relief that Leon has survived the war. Returning from the Pacific in the fall, Leon is among the last troops to be demobilized. He's been gone for four years, and a case of beriberi has left him stiff-legged. Kit bag over his shoulder, he arrives at Union Station in Chicago. Val runs into Leon's arms. Wolfe wraps him in a bear hug, steps back to admire the medals on his chest. Leon shrugs, humble.

Leon is happy to come home to his bride and a job in Wolfe's factory. He is impressed at the sight of Wolfe's new convertible with its shiny chrome trim, the first postwar model. Wolfe looks the part of a fat cat wearing a double-breasted coat and broad-brimmed fedora. Leon senses that something about his brother has changed.

A million is a lot of anything . . . tens of millions is lots more!!!
—Billboard[15]

Wolfe looks down on the deserted factory floor. With the end of World War II, the War Department cancels its orders. The arsenal of democracy goes on surplus sale.

Billboard magazine, known to the trade as the bible of the music industry, reports that nearly every jukebox in the country is broken down and in need of constant repair. There are huge profits to be made replacing more than 500,000 jukeboxes. A lucrative opportunity will soon present itself for Wolfe to fill the demand.

Chicago, July 1946

"I don't know anything about phonographs," Wolfe tells Sam Mannarino, a coin machine operator sitting across the red Naugahyde booth in an Italian restaurant, speckled flecks of gold on the black ceiling above.

Mannarino, forty-five, beefy, shrewd eyes, looks like the late actor James Gandolfini, who portrayed television's fictional suburban gangster Tony Soprano.[16] But Mannarino is the real deal, the king of New Kensington, Pennsylvania. Mannarino grew up on the tough streets of south Pittsburgh. Sam and his younger brother Gabriel, aka "Kelly," started running bootleg liquor as teenagers in the last days of Prohibition. The Mannarinos graduate from the Sicilian Mafia school for survival and make their own New Deal in Depression racketeering.

The Mannarinos run a scrap metal yard, a trucking company, pool halls, nightclubs, and a loan-sharking operation. They become well-known coin men, operating jukeboxes and cigarette and other vending machines. Through bribery, they influence politicians, police officers, and other officials in the Pittsburgh area. They develop close ties with Carlo Gambino, head of one of the five New York families that dominate organized crime nationwide.

Mannarino pours Wolfe another glass of Chianti. He expands on a scheme to invest the millions he rakes in from coin machines into manufacturing jukeboxes.

Wolfe: Why did you come to me?

Mannarino: We heard you were a guy we could do business with.

They size each other up. Jew. Catholic. Both enjoy meatballs and spaghetti. Wear dapper double-breasteds. See the big picture. Men of vision.

Mannarino takes out a set of blueprints. Wolfe inspects the drawings, and with them unfolds the tale of the legendary Filben mechanism.

Small Ideas Have Large Commercial Possibilities!
Should I try to sell my invention before I have it Patented? Is there any safe, business-like way to secure financial help? Can I protect and sell an improvement on some invention that has already been patented? —Modern Mechanix & Invention, *May 1936*[17]

In a shop in St. Paul, Minnesota, William Filben made coin-operated radios for hotels and restaurants. A family man with three daughters, he spent late nights tinkering in his workshop, obsessed with a project that he was convinced would make him rich.

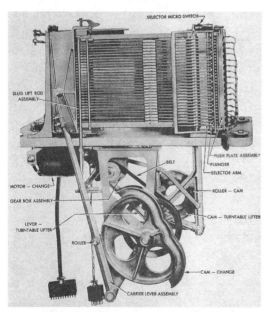

Figure 2.1. The Filben mechanism used in the Maestro jukebox. From the operator's manual.
PUBLIC DOMAIN.

Filben built a jukebox with a phonograph changer that could hold thirty records, far more than the leading models from the manufacturers that dominated the market, Rock-ola, Seeburg, and WurliTzer. His machine had fewer moving parts and would be more reliable.

The hard-drinking Irish American assembled each unit by hand, placed them in local bars and restaurants, and serviced them himself. But the stress of building machines, running the routes, and managing the business was too much for the forty-three-year-old independent. He died of a heart attack in 1940, leaving everything to his wife and three little girls.

The inventor's death, followed by the wartime injunction on jukebox manufacturing, thwarted plans to go into production. With the end of World War II, the restrictions were lifted, and the Filben family formed a company to capitalize on the inventor's legacy. They struck a deal for the manufacturing rights with Batavia Metal Products, a company near Chicago controlled by the brother industrialists Henry and Murray Garsson. Just as the first jukebox to incorporate Filben's mechanism was introduced, the Garssons were indicted by the Justice Department for manufacturing defective artillery shells and wartime profiteering. The Batavia plant closed, and the deal to manufacture the Filben jukebox was dead. For the inventor's straitlaced family, it would be their introduction to the cutthroat world of the coin machine industry.

Wolfe: Strange coincidence. I had a call today from a salesman at Batavia. Something about a phonograph.

Mannarino: I wouldn't do business with those scumbags.

He waves a contract at Wolfe. He made the widow an offer she had to take. Now he has the rights to the Filben name and patents.

Mannarino: I need a man who can go into production.

Wolfe leafs through the plans again. Schematics for a phonograph that can select a record, place it on a turntable, and replace it in the stack after play. With a capacity of thirty records, it could revolutionize the jukebox industry.

Wolfe: Have you shown these to anyone else?
Mannarino: This is the Holy Grail. It's worth millions.

Mannarino offers a partnership. Fifty-fifty. Wolfe will be responsible for manufacturing the jukebox. Mannarino will control distribution and sales.

Wolfe shares the prospect with Trudy. But she is concerned about control. "You've always been your own man," she counsels. He draws on his cigar, considering.

New Deal
Winnipeg, August 7, 1946
Wolfe flies to Winnipeg with a heavy heart. His father has passed away. The death of David "Doc" Rabinovitch, the little Jew from Ternovke in Ukraine who pioneered on the Manitoba prairies before electricity, automobiles, telephones, and radio, marks the end of an era. His mother Sonia weeps. Old men with long beards wearing hats and prayer shawls chant the ritual Hebraic incantations.

Doc's four sons, Archie, Wolfe, Milton, and Leon, and two grandsons carry the blue wood casket with the Star of David from the living room down the steps through a throng of family and friends to the Cadillac hearse waiting at the curb to take the funeral party to the cemetery.

Wolfe stays for two days of *shiva*,[18] but there are continual calls from Chicago, and he needs to take care of business. Milt assures him Doc would understand. Wolfe kisses his mother good-bye. She hugs him and whispers in his ear, "My son, the big shot."

Chicago, November 27, 1946

You didn't take me to the Stork Club
You took me to the stork.
Oh Mr. Siegel, make it legal,
Mr. Fink, please make it mink!

—"Mr. Siegel, Make It Legal," written by Jack Yellen[19]

On stage at the Chez Paree, a ritzy Chicago supper club, Sophie Tucker performs hits from a repertoire considered risqué for its time. Champagne flows at the Rabin table. Wolfe has flown his brother Milton and bride Sheila to Chicago for their honeymoon. Milt's wife is a petite blue-eyed brunette, a nice Jewish girl his mother approves of. She drinks too much trying to keep up with her new sister-in-law Trudy.

After the show, Wolfe escorts Sophie, "the last of the red-hot mamas," to the table. The entertainer does a double take on seeing Leon, mistakes him for Jimmy Cagney.[20] You were wonderful in *Yankee Doodle Dandy*, she effuses. She autographs a copy of her memoirs for the bride and groom, "To Mr. and Mrs. Milton Rabin, Heartiest Congratulations."

Coin man Sam Mannarino stops by Wolfe's table. When Wolfe introduces him as a prospective business partner, Trudy's face tightens. Does Wolfe realize whom he is getting in bed with?

"Got a new deal," Wolfe confides to Milt. "Could be the biggest thing since sliced bread. Maybe I can get you in on it." Milt cocks an eyebrow, intrigued.

Mannarino bites into a hot pastrami sandwich at Schwartz's Delicatessen. Wolfe urges him to try the chopped liver. The table is littered with napkins covered with calculations scribbled in pencil. Mannarino wants to know what it will cost to go into production. Manufacturing jukeboxes requires a substantial industrial operation, on the order of assembling an automobile. Wolfe's budget comes to $240,000—about $10 million today.

They shake hands on a deal to build a prototype for a jukebox based on the Filben mechanism. Half a million jukeboxes need to be replaced across the country. All the incentive Wolfe needs.

Despite a lack of formal training, Wolfe is brilliant at electrical engineering. When it comes to assembling the phonograph mechanism, the drawings Mannarino had given him leave a lot to be desired. The inventor's design is flawed.

With Leon at his side, he rewires the circuitry for the prototype. They reassemble the record selector, turntable, control panel, and coin changer.

The mechanism engages. Wolfe stares, mesmerized, watching the changer load and unload discs in sequence, over and over. Leon suggests they brand it the Rabin.

They name it the Stowaway because it has no case or speaker. Connected to coin-operated remote controls in restaurant booths and speakers on the wall, the changer unit can be hidden from sight, permitting easy access for service.

Milwaukee, February 6, 1947

Coin men get their own section in *Billboard*, bestowing the industry with legitimacy and the glamour of showbiz. Wolfe and Leon are about to enter the real world of the coin men. Distributors from across the Midwest wheel and deal in the smoke-filled showroom of the United Coin Machine Company. Hit songs blare from competing jukeboxes.

The debut of the Stowaway rates the cover story in *Coin Machine Review*. The prototype attracts interest from independent operators. Because the Stowaway has no cabinet, it is less expensive than the competition and provides easier access to change the record lineup for mom-and-pop operators who service the jukeboxes themselves.

Seeing that Wolfe and Leon are new, Lefty Korman, an independent from Milwaukee,[21] offers some friendly advice on the rules for coin men.

> Lefty: If you want to sell, you have got to get a union sticker on your jukebox. Call up the girl at the operators' association office. See if the buyer is on the courtesy list.

But Korman's advice barely registers with Wolfe, who is busy directing the newsreel cameras.

The coin man turns to Leon with a warning.

> Lefty: If you're in the association, they've got an agreement not to solicit each other's locations. Pays to check. That way nobody gets hurt, see.

Ten years later, a U.S. Senate committee will expose the methods used by racketeers to take over the jukebox industry.

> *The majority of persons in this field are, we believe, honest, legitimate businessmen and workers. However, they have frequently found themselves hampered and restricted by arrangements between competitors and by unscrupulous union officials. Also, to an increasing degree, they have been forced to deal with racketeers and to pay tribute to them for the right to stay in business.*[22]

Chapter Three

Coin Men

Partners
Chicago, February 1947
Smoking in the loge at the Orpheum, Wolfe and Leon sit
between their wives, whose enmity is palpable. But they can't contain
their excitement when Wolfe appears ten feet high on screen in the
newsreel demonstrating the latest in jukebox technology.

Wolfe: We're going to be bigger than WurliTzer!
The newsreel continues.

Garssons Indicted for War Profiteering!
Shots of a boarded up industrial facility. Men in overcoats and
hats shielding their faces arrive at the Department of Justice in
Washington, DC. A silver-haired man with the profile of a Roman
senator speaks to the camera.

Newsreel Announcer: Batavia Metal Works has declared
bankruptcy and its owners, Murray and Henry Garsson have been
charged with profiteering on $78 million in war contracts. The
former Attorney General of Pennsylvania, Charles Margiotti, will
defend the accused profiteers.

Chicago, February 20, 1947

The intercom buzzes in Wolfe's office. Call from Charles Margiotti in Pittsburgh. Wolfe recognizes his caller's name from the newsreel. The former attorney general of Pennsylvania is defense counsel for the notorious Garsson brothers, indicted for wartime profiteering.

Wolfe is suspicious. What has the profiteering case got to do with him? Nothing to do with that, the caller assures him.

Margiotti has a formidable reputation. As a young prosecutor, he secured the conviction of the first woman to be executed in Pennsylvania. Margiotti was the highest official of Italian American heritage ever elected in the state when he became attorney general. On leaving office, he crossed the bar, successfully defending 149 accused murderers! But the portly, bespectacled lawyer has not forgotten his ties to the old neighborhood. He is consigliere to the Mannarino family, advising on business matters, defending them from indictments, and acting as front man in legitimate businesses.

Margiotti explains to Wolfe that he represents Sam Mannarino's syndicate, the investors with the money that Wolfe needs to go into production. But there's a catch. The men putting up the money want to own the company. They would like Wolfe to be the president and run the operation. Margiotti will be the chairman of the board. Mannarino will take care of distribution. Since Wolfe is in Chicago, he can incorporate the company. As Wolfe is the sole owner, he can issue stock in the company, and no public filing will be required.

Trudy's words echo in Wolfe's ears. "Be your own man." But he rationalizes the deal as a production contract. He is not on the hook; he simply has to build the machines. As long as he gets his cut off the top, he will get rich.

Wolfe registers the Filben Company, using the trade name for the mechanism. He leases factory space in an industrial building on South Wabash Avenue. He envisions assembly lines and offices for shipping, administration, sales, and marketing.

Mannarino's bagman Max Goldberg arrives from Pittsburgh. A fussy accountant with a moustache, he takes bundles of cash from his attaché case, stacks them on Wolfe's desk. Start-up funds.

Trudy enters without knocking, exclaims at seeing the pile of money on Wolfe's desk.

"From the investors," Goldberg explains.

Trudy turns on Wolfe. He has a lot of explaining to do. Trudy is furious that Wolfe has sold out. She doesn't trust his new business partners. She doesn't want to see him get hurt.

"I can handle them," he assures her.

Wolfe appoints Leon production manager, and the brothers build the company overnight. They hire electricians, mechanics, engineers, and woodworkers, all World War II veterans. Wolfe selects an African American foreman, Fergus, a burly vet who wears a Masonic pin and calls him Brother Wolfe. When the American Legion learns of his hiring policy, they hold a ceremony to honor Wolfe and present him with a certificate of appreciation.

A cheer rises as the first Stowaway completes its journey along the assembly line. Five units are crated and wheeled to the loading dock. Leon affixes the shipping labels to Lefty Korman at the United Coin Machine Company in Milwaukee.

Figure 3.1. Trade advertisement for Filben "Mirrocle" jukebox. Note Stowaway unit, no cabinet, lower left. Published in *Billboard*, 1947. PUBLIC DOMAIN.

Over on the West Side of Chicago, a record shatters against an office wall. David Rockola has just been informed that the Stowaway is in production, and he is furious.

Rockola, forty-nine, now rules an eponymous empire that spans four city blocks. He added a hyphen to the company name, calling it Rock-ola, which sounded impressive, like Victrola, the phonograph maker, or Motorola, the car radio company.

If it took coins to operate, Rock-ola produced it, from pinball games to parking meters and gumball machines. When Rock-ola began manufacturing a coin-operated phonograph, the founder had an epiphany. Music would be the most profitable product to sell on coin machines—if the technology could be developed.

As though playing the popular new board game Monopoly, Rockola acquired patents in lieu of real estate. He cornered the market on the rights to parts for a record changer and went into production in 1935. The Rock-ola Model A, encased in a four-foot-high wooden cabinet with the changer visible, was the first jukebox to offer a selection from twelve discs, and it set off a frenzy of competition.

By 1947, Rock-ola Manufacturing employs more than three thousand workers who make twenty-five thousand jukeboxes annually, about a quarter of the American market.

Rockola stomps across the factory, inspecting the assembly line. He notices some parts lying on the floor, turns on a worker, and demands, "Would you throw money away like this at home?"

David Rockola probes the workings of the Stowaway record changer on the workbench. He suspects that the Stowaway is not wholly original. He dissects the machine for evidence of patent infringement.

After the Chicago Coin Machine Show in 1938, Rockola had gone to St. Paul, Minnesota, to check out William Filben's operation, which turned out to be two small rooms with workbenches. When he examined the new phonograph, he found that the "inventor" had incorporated some of Rockola's patented parts. Although not entirely original, Filben's mechanism offered some innovations, notably the thirty-disc changer.

Shrewdly, the jukebox pioneer proposed an exchange of patent rights. Rock-ola, with its industrial capacity, would manufacture the jukebox, paying a royalty on sales to Filben. The inventor would retain the right to produce the mechanism and operate it using his own name. They made the deal, but Filben assembled only a handful of jukeboxes before being stricken with a heart attack. Then World War II intervened.

The War Production Board had declared a moratorium on manufacturing jukeboxes in 1942, and the Rock-ola Corporation converted to manufacturing M1 rifles, a contract that would be worth $40 million. By 1946, the project to manufacture a jukebox using the Filben mechanism isn't even on the drawing board; in fact, David Rockola sees the value in keeping it off the market. He hadn't contemplated that the inventor's family would form a corporation to exploit the rights.[1]

Rockola aims to choke the competition over the rights to the Filben mechanism. Alleging patent infringement, he files suit against the inventor's widow, Bernice Filben, forty-five, and her daughters. At issue are three patents for the multi-selector unit and one patent used in the changer mechanism.

Minneapolis, April 1947

The *Rockola v. Filben* case begins in U.S. District Court in Minneapolis. While Wolfe Rabin isn't named in the suit, the outcome could pose a dire threat to his nascent manufacturing operation.

Rockola's team of patent attorneys flies in from Chicago, briefcases spilling over with patents and memoranda as they annex one side of the courtroom. The defense of the inventor's heirs has fallen to Len Baskfield, forty-five, a local lawyer who had filed Filben's patent claims and written his will. When the Filben family appears—the inventor's widow, Bernice, forty-five, with her daughters Rosemary, seventeen; Patricia, fifteen; and Dolores, thirteen—a reporter seizes on the "David vs. Goliath" angle. He files a story portraying the inventor's small-town family victimized by a wealthy industrialist.

David Rockola takes the stand, testifying to the dominance of the jukebox industry cartel.

The WurliTzer Company, our company, and the J.P. Seeburg Corporation manufacture approximately 85 per cent of the jukeboxes that are made in this country. As far as our own company is concerned, we *manufacture approximately 25 per cent of that. Our volume will be somewhere in the neighborhood of $10 million a year.*[2]

Stumbling as he begins, Baskfield makes an impassioned plea for the rights and compensation due to the inventor's widow and children. But the judge's ruling will rest on interpretation of the law as to whether rights conveyed by patent license are personal to the licensee.

JUKEBOX WARS
Chicago, September 5, 1947

Wolfe tears a sheet off the telex printer, reads the decision hot off the wire in the patent infringement suit. The judge has ruled that the inventor's heirs had the right to organize a corporation, to assign their rights to that corporation, and were empowered to vest another corporation with the right to manufacture phonographs using the Filben brand name. The judgment removes the cloud hanging over Wolfe's company.

David Rockola instructs his lawyers to appeal the decision. But the distributors of Rock-ola jukeboxes are losing patience. The Stowaways are selling into their territories. Wolfe hadn't heeded Korman's warning that infringing on the cartel's locations would have consequences. Rival syndicates send their goons to threaten, picket, and disrupt the stops where operators have installed the Stowaway.

Chicago, January 1948

In a downtown Chicago bar, a boogie-woogie thumps from an unseen jukebox. Two men enter. One pulls out a gun, the second wields an axe. The patrons freeze. The men demand to see the jukebox. The bartender opens a cabinet, revealing a Filben Stowaway. The man with the axe bashes the jukebox while his partner holds off the crowd with his gun. The music skips and stops.

Milwaukee, January 1948

Three men with handkerchiefs covering their faces enter the showroom of the United Coin Machine Company. Behind the counter, Lefty Korman reaches for his gun. The men draw their guns and fire repeatedly at the coin man. He falls to the floor, his body riddled with bullets. They shoot up the jukeboxes on display, then flee the showroom.

Opposing the mob's dominance over coin machine revenues results in beatings, kidnappings, and abductions. The jukebox wars stay in the headlines and on the radio news for the next fifteen years. "Slain Juke Racket Rival Feared Bomb," screams one front page banner, reporting the gruesome account of a St. Louis jukebox distributor slain in a hail of bullets.[3]

The victims are coin men, Wolfe's new friends. Lucky Lefty Korman somehow survived nine bullet wounds. He thinks about Korman's warning.

Wolfe needs protection.

The foreman Fergus interrupts with a collect call from Mr. Leon in St. Louis. Urgent. Wolfe picks up.

Leon: They told me I better not leave the hotel. They told me they would kill me if I tried to leave.

Wolfe: Where are they?

Leon: In the lobby.

Wolfe: Did you get the order for the east side?

Leon: That's what got me into this jam.

The line goes dead.

Wolfe stubs out his cigarette, slides another Lucky Strike from the pack, lights it, depresses the switch to get a line. The operator comes on.

Wolfe: Person to person for Sam Mannarino in Pittsburgh.

He needs to ask a favor.

Later that evening, the telephone rings in Wolfe's penthouse suite. Collect from Leon. He walked through the hotel lobby. The goons were gone. He has a ticket on the evening train to Chicago. A wave of relief passes through Wolfe. He pours a shot of Johnny Walker.

Crosslake, Minnesota, June 9, 1947

"You can get your kicks, on Route 66." Wolfe snaps his fingers to Nat King Cole's hit song playing on the radio of a black Chrysler cruising along a two-lane road in northern Minnesota. The turret lens of Wolfe's

16mm points out the window, capturing shaky images of the giant statues of Paul Bunyan and the Blue Ox rushing by.

Sam Mannarino lifts a hand from the wheel, draws on his cigar. Mannarino reveals that he has been watching Wolfe since they got into business together.

> Mannarino: You never throw any curve balls.
> Wolfe: That way I never have to catch any.

Mannarino punches him playfully on the shoulder, says he will introduce Wolfe to the players at the jukebox summit.

The big car winds through clusters of rustic cabins amid the pine trees dotting the rolling grounds of the Whitefish Resort. Lincolns and Cadillacs with license plates from a dozen states fill the parking lot. Drivers in dark suits wearing Ray-Bans hang by the vehicles, smoking, wary.

At the main lodge, Wolfe and Mannarino are greeted by the vice president for the rival WurliTzer Company, Milton Hammergren, who owns the resort. Assigned to share cabins like teenagers at a summer camp,[4] more than fifty coin men have come to iron out their differences.

Mannarino points out a short man in Bermuda shorts and knee-high socks. "That's 'Greasy Thumb' Guzik," Mannarino confides. "Used to be Capone's bagman. Now he is a distributor."

At the shuffleboard court, two men are taking bets on the sideline. "Two of your tribe," Mannarino tells Wolfe, introducing him to Meyer Lansky's partners Al Goldberg and Willie Blye.

When they are not pointing guns at each other, Wolfe observes, these guys are okay.

Mannarino is eager to grab a shotgun and go duck hunting. But business comes first. In nonstop running dialogues, territories are carved out, deals made. A cease-fire is called, putting an end to the bloodshed over jukeboxes, for the time being.

BREAKTHROUGH

The demand for the Stowaway is driven by technology and design. The thirty-song record selector and hidden remote-controlled phonograph changer are breakthroughs. But a jukebox without a cabinet has limited appeal to location owners who want a visual showcase for the music. Wolfe needs a full product line, a stand-alone model in a cabinet to complement the bare-bones Stowaway. Now with Mannarino's backing, he can take on the big manufacturers who introduce new models every year.

Wolfe sketches. He designs a jukebox like none other. No wood, all chrome and hard plastics, a streamlined look for the postwar era. The futuristic cabinet encloses a changer and selector with improved electronics, amplification, and speakers. He assembles a prototype, names it the Maestro '48.

Hostesses greet coin men gathering in a Chicago hotel penthouse for the introduction of the Maestro. Rumor spreads that the jukebox was designed by Raymond Loewy, the master of American indus-

trial design.[5] The fantastic Maestro is Wolfe's baby, and its striking design and state-of-the-art technology result in a jukebox phenomenon. Orders come to an astonishing $42 million.[6]

Wolfe's manufacturing operation expands through six floors of the building on South Wabash. More than 200 men and women work long shifts assembling jukeboxes. "Filben Music Line Output Reaches Peak," exclaims *Billboard*.[7]

Mannarino and Goldberg, his bagman, hunch over Wolfe's desk. While the accountant reviews the ledgers, Mannarino counts stacks of cash into bundles.

Figure 3.2. The Maestro jukebox. Wolfe's revolutionary music machine that played thirty discs. PUBLIC DOMAIN.

The Black foreman Fergus pokes his head in the door, sees the cash on the desk, backs away.

Mannarino: Can you trust him?

Wolfe: He's a lodge brother.

Mannarino passes Wolfe several bundles of cash. Wolfe wheels his chair over to the safe, puts the money inside, closes the safe, spins the lock. He works behind what lawyers call a "Chinese wall." There are some questions it is better not to ask. There are some things that you don't want to know.

Wolfe spends money as fast as it comes in. Diamond earrings and furs for Trudy. A gold watch for Leon. Flashy cars. A penthouse suite. Living the high life. Captured on 16mm Kodachrome by the roving eye of Wolfe's turret-lens Bell & Howell.

Leon is troubled by the source of this wealth but accepts Wolfe's largesse and looks the other way.

Figure 3.3. Wolfe and brother Milton, circa 1947. Wolfe counts $1,000 bills to give to his brother Milton to take to Canada "for a rainy day." COPYRIGHT THE AUTHOR.

Sitting across a wooden desk in his office, Wolfe counts fifty $1,000 bills, hands them to his brother Milton with instructions to take the money back to Canada "for a rainy day." Milt puts the stack of bills in a small strongbox. Leon takes a photograph, capturing the moment with the money on the table. A bemused expression crosses Wolfe's face.

Milt takes the money for safekeeping but offers some advice. There will be a day of reckoning, he warns. There could be an audit. Might be a good idea to invest in government bonds for security.

Minneapolis, April 26, 1948

The latest "bubbler" model jukeboxes featuring flashing lights around burled wood cabinets add to the carnival-like atmosphere of the Northwest Coin Machine Show. Thousands come to check out the state of the art in machine culture from jukebox vendors, game, record, and needle distributors. The major jukebox manufacturers, WurliTzer, Rock-ola, and Seeburg, each with their own racketeering affiliations among the distributors, erect walk-in displays. Hostesses solicit operators to preview the latest models.

A burly man in a gray suit glad-hands his way through the convention hall. Senator Homer Earl Capehart, fifty-one, a conservative Republican from Indiana, is there to deliver the keynote address. He strides to the podium, waves to the crowd of coin men.

> *Jukeboxes can now become a great and timely answer to any despoilers of our ideals and of our liberty. The jukebox is a solution to the delinquency that affects our youth. We should build entertainment centers to keep adolescents off the streets. —Senator Homer Capehart*[8]

Capehart promotes the jukebox as a wholesome solution to juvenile delinquency. The industrialist rails against the influence of organized crime in the coin-operated music industry, ironic since he has his own ties to the Mob.

Capehart has a personal stake in the battle for jukebox supremacy. He receives a royalty for the Simplex selector used in every WurliTzer jukebox and immediately perceives Wolfe Rabin and the Maestro as a threat to the jukebox cartel.[9]

As the son of a frugal Indiana farmer, young Homer experienced strong doses of family affection, Christian teaching, and backbreaking work on a tenant farm.[10] In the 1920s, Capehart bounced around the Midwest, selling milking machines, tractors, and plows. He made good money as a salesman for Butterkist popcorn machines, an American icon with no competition. Commissioned sales supported Capehart's young family. But he was looking for a big score.

In 1927, a small-time inventor named Thomas Small showed Capehart his invention, an automatic record changer that played one side of a stack of records, turned the stack over, and played the other side.[11] Capehart gambled his savings to acquire the patents.

In the enterprising spirit of the Jazz Age, Capehart's start-up attracted partners and investors. The Automatic Phonograph Corporation opened its factory in Fort Wayne, Indiana, in 1929. It was a substantial industrial operation employing three hundred workers. Sales were brisk. With high-quality sound, Capehart became known as the "Steinway" of the phonograph industry.

The Roaring Twenties ended with the stock market crash of October 29, 1929. So did Homer Capehart's fledgling company, hounded by creditors.

Capehart was down but not out. He came across a small company called Simplex, which had developed a device that allowed a person to select the record to be played from an automatic record changer. The Multi-Selector allowed customers to insert a nickel and select a particular record to listen to on a phonograph rather than only being able to listen to records play in the order in which they were stacked. This was a major innovation. Capehart acquired the patent rights. The Multi-Selector would be the engine for his big idea. He would make the device coin operated.

With the Depression at its nadir, in 1933, Capehart rides the train to North Tonawanda, New York, alighting at the headquarters of the Rudolph WurliTzer Company, the manufacturer of organs, pianos, and radios. It is the largest woodworking, metalworking, and assembly plant in the world devoted to the production of musical instruments. The half-mile-long plant is situated on a forty-four-acre campus and consumes 10 million board feet of lumber annually. But the maker of the

Mighty WurliTzer organ for movie palaces had fallen on hard times with the advent of "talking pictures."

An ebullient Capehart presents the plans for the coin-operated Simplex selector. Desperate for a new product to replace its fading line of coin-operated player pianos, Farny WurliTzer, son of the company founder Rudolph, makes a deal with Capehart to manufacture the new phonographs—which will soon become known as jukeboxes. Capehart joins WurliTzer Music as vice president and general sales manager.

Introduced in 1933, the Debutante jukebox stands in a five-foot-high wooden cabinet, weighs two hundred pounds, plays ten discs, and can make change for a quarter. With competitors from Rock-ola, the J. P. Seeburg Company, and others, the new music machines become a phenomenon in the middle of the Great Depression.

Homer Capehart combines WurliTzer's national network of dealers with his own rolodex of connections. A young racketeer from New York becomes one of Capehart's key distributors. Meyer Lansky heads a syndicate that is making a fortune from illegal gambling and bookmaking operations in South Florida. With an enormous cash flow that needs to be laundered, Lansky sees the potential of jukeboxes as a useful front and a profit center themselves. In 1937, he signs with WurliTzer as the Simplex distributor for South Florida.

WurliTzer's jukebox sales rocket from three thousand units in 1933 to more than twenty-five thousand annually by 1939. The "WurliTzer Arch" would soon become second only to the Coke bottle as the most recognized trademark worldwide.

Homer Capehart is profiled in *Fortune* as "one of the highest-powered, highest-pressure salesmen this country has ever produced. . . . His manner is expansive, his personality is forward, winning, and often overwhelming."[12] With his personal wealth assured, Capehart begins to develop an interest in politics.

Capehart credits his success to hard work, individual self-discipline, and an optimistic attitude, and he felt that both the Republican Party and the American nation needed a good dose of those qualities[13] to recover from the recession and what he saw as the socialist policies of FDR's New Deal.

August 27, 1938. An estimated twenty thousand people drive or take the train to Capehart's Indiana farm for the great "Cornfield Conference."

"Twenty-eight blue and white striped tents were arranged on a 120 acre freshly mowed alfalfa field. One large tent held ten thousand people seated at tables; other tents held state delegations, kitchens, radio broadcasters and the press, first aid and concessions."[14]

Capehart's sales experience informs his oratory. He charges that

> *Roosevelt has spellbound his believers into feeling that the Republican Party is interested in only . . . the reduction of taxes; the piling up of profit for private enterprise and the protection and ownership of property . . . that when Republicans get into power again they will not take care of the unemployed and will champion NO social legislation.*

He rejects this reasoning and identifies Republicanism with Americanism,[15] asserting that "we are not yet a Communistic country, nor a Socialistic country, nor a Nazi country, nor a Fascist country. We cannot live under two systems of government, the American system and the New Deal experiment."[16]

Billboard reports that should Capehart "run as a candidate thousands of admiring coin machine men will be plugging for him to win."[17]

Buoyed by the populist enthusiasm of the Cornfield Conference, Capehart cashes out his stake in WurliTzer to finance a political campaign. Elected senator from Indiana in 1944, he is in position to secure substantial contracts to manufacture parts for the army and navy during World War II.

WurliTzer's slogan is "The Phonograph of Tomorrow," but the big news at the Northwest Coin Machine Show is Wolfe and his Maestro '48, the jet-age newcomer with the biggest record capacity. David Rockola sends agents to snoop around the booth where Wolfe and Leon are racking up sales for the Maestro.

Facing this new competition, the WurliTzer Company promises twenty-one gigantic stopover parties for operators who ride the WurliTzer Transcontinental Limited, a coast-to-coast luxury train. Wolfe won't be out done. He negotiates with the air force to buy a surplus plane, a twin-engine fourteen-seat Lockheed Lodestar, and paints "Maestro" on the cowl. He barnstorms the country with a planeload of distributors, operators, and cronies, drawing newsreel cameras everywhere he lands, from Nashville to Little Rock, Omaha, Des Moines, up through the south to Roanoke and Baltimore. Orders flood the telex back to Chicago, where Leon supervises production at the ever-expanding plant.

Pittsburgh, July 1948

Wolfe enjoys rubbing shoulders with the stars. He stages a promotion at Forbes Field, home of baseball's Pittsburgh Pirates. A Maestro stands on the pitcher's mound. Two of America's most-worshipped celebrities are there to endorse Wolfe's jukebox.

Hank Greenberg, the "Hebrew Hammer," the returning war hero who has just signed the richest contract in baseball history,[18] introduces his pal who needs no introduction, the perennial number one on every jukebox, Bing Crosby. The crowd goes wild.

Greenberg prods Crosby, a closet gambler and notable tightwad, to take a nickel from his pocket to play the novelty song they had recorded together with comedian Groucho Marx.

> Oh, goodbye, Mr. Ball, goodbye
> You had better kiss your relatives goodbye
> When Hank comes to the plate, Ball,
> You're gonna to be out late so
> Goodbye, Mr. Ball, goodbye!
>
> —"Goodbye, Mr. Ball,"
> written by Bill Coryn and Harold Smith

Jukeboxes consume 67 million records in 1947, estimated as one-third of all recordings produced.[19] The distributors decide whose records are placed in the jukeboxes, which position they occupy on the index, and which singer's recordings should be put in the number one position. Jukebox play can make an American idol.

The group in the owner's box for the game that afternoon includes Wolfe, Sam Mannarino, Mannarino's consigliere Charles Margiotti, and Bing Crosby.

Linking the relationships in the box at Forbes Field that afternoon, there is an unspoken partner.

Mannarino's syndicate owns Wolfe's jukebox company, with Margiotti as chairman.

The syndicate also owns a piece of the Pittsburgh Pirates, with Margiotti as director.

And a piece of Bing Crosby's record sales.

Music and baseball. Entertainment and sports. American businesses falling under the control of organized crime.

In 1947, the jukebox empire rakes in nickels, dimes, and quarters to the tune of more than $10 million a week.

CARTEL

Wolfe slams the telephone on his desk. The subcontractors refuse to ship machine parts he needs to assemble the Maestro. Rock-ola has taken their entire output. Same story when he calls another supplier who informs him that WurliTzer has contracted for their production. "Fucking restraint of trade," he explodes.

The only way to break the competition's lock on the parts is to create custom tool and die work. Wolfe proposes to build a foundry. But where will he get the money?

Leon clutches a fistful of orders. "We can do it ourselves."

Wolfe makes an appointment at his bank. The brothers set up the prototype in the bank manager's office. Wolfe puts a nickel in the slot, selects a song. When the music plays, everyone in the bank gathers. The tellers begin to dance. The demonstration is convincing.

The bank manager asks Wolfe if he has prepared a business plan. He drops a stack of orders on the manager's desk. But the bank requires financial documents, and he doesn't have the time for the bureaucratic process.

Reluctantly, he turns to his patron. Mannarino asks how much money Wolfe needs. With a pencil on a napkin, Wolfe calculates a budget. Clears his throat. Shows it to Mannarino. He needs a lot of money to tool up.

Mannarino flicks the ash from his cigar into the ashtray. He agrees to advance the funds as a loan.

The bagman Goldberg delivers more cash. With the money, Wolfe builds a foundry on the outskirts of Chicago to produce parts for the Maestro. He surveys the operation with satisfaction, the orange glow of molten metal reflecting on his face.

If only Doc could see him now. He feels invincible. But the jukebox impresario is standing on a precipice.

St. Paul, January 28, 1949

Rock-ola wins its appeal in the patent infringement suit. The appeal court rules that William Filben's heirs violated Rock-ola's rights by licensing and contracting manufacturing of the mechanism to others. The Filben family's request for a rehearing is denied. Their lawyer Baskfield files an appeal to the Supreme Court.

Rockola names Wolfe's company in eight patent infringement suits filed simultaneously in Chicago, Denver, Miami, Milwaukee, and San Francisco. Wolfe is now in the line of fire, along with the entire manufacturing, distribution, and sales setup. Rockola demands an injunction and millions in damages. Wolfe confers with Charles Margiotti, the former Pennsylvania attorney general turned Mob lawyer.

Wolfe works the phones, damage control with the distributors. The coin men are sympathetic, but they don't need the heat. Wolfe reassures them that their loyalty will be rewarded. A reporter from *Billboard* calls. Wolfe confidently tells him that "all the Filben distributors have been advised of the latest legal moves, and that all the distributors were thoroly [*sic*] behind Filben."[20]

Chicago, February 17, 1949

Wolfe is subpoenaed to testify. Riding the elevator to the offices of the Rock-ola Company's lawyers to be deposed, Wolfe steels himself for the encounter with his nemesis, David Rockola. "Just another country boy from Manitoba," he reminds himself.

But the confrontation never takes place. David Rockola, the litigious jukebox pioneer, doesn't show up. Across a conference table, Wolfe confronts the plaintiff's white-haired counsel Tom Sheridan, seventy-four, who demands to know who owns the Filben Corporation.

Sheridan: Who were the subscribing stockholders?

Wolfe: The stock was subscribed by one individual as trustee for all the stockholders.

One stock certificate was made to this Max Goldberg as trustee for all the stockholders.

Sheridan: Who were the stockholders?

Wolfe draws on his Monte Cristo, slowly exhales.

Wolfe: To tell you the truth, Mr. Sheridan, I don't know to this day who all the stockholders are.

There are some questions it is better not to ask. There are some things you don't want to know.

Sheridan: Do you know whether any reports were made to Sam Mannarino?

Answer the truth. Nothing to hide.

Wolfe: Sam Mannarino received his reports, yes. He would come in and get those reports personally.

Sheridan persists in attempting to make a connection to the Pittsburgh coin man. But Wolfe is confident that Mannarino's name does not appear in any documents.

Sheridan: Is he a stockholder in the Filben Corporation?

Remember the Chinese wall.

Wolfe: That I can't answer.

Sheridan smokes a cigarette, frustrated.

Sheridan: Now, what information were you given when they gave your company a license to manufacture these Filben phonographs?

Wolfe leans forward, ready to explain.

Wolfe: I was shown some patent papers, under the name of William Filben. I was shown the decision of the Court giving his heirs the rights to either manufacture or have the jukebox manufactured for them, and—
Sheridan: In other words, you were advised that you had a legal right—
Wolfe: —to manufacture for them, or whoever they designated.[21]

But the proceedings in Chicago are moot. The Supreme Court issues a writ of a certiorari, denying Baskfield's appeal in Rockola's patent infringement case. The licensing agreement Mannarino had shown Wolfe is void.

Federal marshals arrive at Wolfe's plant, flash their badges, spread around the factory floor. A marshal reads the injunction.

Marshal: You are to desist and refrain from the further manufacture and sale of phonographs and selector mechanisms in infringement of Letters Patent No. 16-3785.

Leon rushes to the loading dock, urging the men to get a shipment of crated jukeboxes into vans. A van pulls off as agents arrive.

Amid the confusion, Wolfe climbs up on a table, calls for attention.

Wolfe: We won the war and we thought that anything was possible. But if you try to buck the system, the big guys and the politicians get together to come down on you. You have all worked hard and you've been loyal but it's tough to compete against power and influence.

The workers cheer. But when they return to their stations, the marshals intervene. Production shuts down, the workers are laid off. They have produced more than 900 Stowaways and 1,100 Maestros.[22]

The next day, the floor is empty, quiet. Just Wolfe and Trudy, Leon, the foreman Fergus, in a smoke-filled office, phones ringing with creditors. Orders that can't be filled. Piles of bills. Jukeboxes stand in wooden crates at the dock waiting to ship.

In Washington, D.C., Senator Homer Capehart calls David Rockola to congratulate him on his victory in the patent infringement case. Rockola thanks his rival for briefing the court on the jukebox industry. Bitter rivals briefly allied against the common threat.

Ten years later, when Senator Capehart sits on a Senate committee investigating the coin machine industry, he frequently sends an aide for briefings by the committee counsel, Robert Kennedy.

"I was asked whether we were observing due process," Kennedy writes, "and whether witnesses were being treated in a way that Senator Capehart would approve. I was courteous, but the aide's visits suddenly ceased. I subsequently learned why: he had been indicted in New York for tampering with a witness."[23]

With the company collapsing, Wolfe is concerned about his outstanding debt to Mannarino, the loan he used to build the foundry.

Mannarino: You can forget about it. And I'll forget about it. But some day I might remember. You know what I mean?

Wolfe: Someday you're going to need the money.

Mannarino: More like a favor.

Mannarino offers Wolfe a job. Come work for him. He is going to sell slot machines to the casinos in Cuba.

The offer is tempting. But Trudy sees the opportunity for Wolfe to get clear of the Mob. "You've done your deal with the devil," she tells him. She slides onto his lap, wraps her arms around his neck, and offers him a choice. "The devil, or me," she whispers in his ear.

Trudy is right. He has got to be his own man. He goes back to the drawing board. He sketches. "High fidelity," he tells Leon. "A stereo in every home. It's going to be the next big thing!"

But once the mob has a piece of your soul, it is like a mortgage that can never be paid off.

CHAPTER FOUR

Crime Busters

AT THE HEIGHT OF THE POST–WORLD WAR II JUKEBOX BOOM, THERE are an estimated eight thousand operators in the United States running more than half a million jukeboxes. Throughout the country, the pattern of underworld infiltration is mushrooming.[1]

Big-time operators have hundreds of stops, employing aspiring tough guys to collect the cash and service the machines. Some Mafia soldiers earn a living as vending machine repairmen.[2]

Just as Wolfe Rabin leaves the jukebox industry, a reform-minded senator from Tennessee determines to rip the lid off the coin machine rackets. Tall and upright with a reputation for integrity, Senator Estes Kefauver chairs the Special Committee to Investigate Organized Crime in Interstate Commerce. In 1950–1951, Kefauver and his committee travel the country, holding hearings and forcing gangsters to testify under subpoena in fourteen cities. Live television is in its infancy, and local stations find the novelty of broadcasting gangsters testifying in front of the senators drawing record-breaking audiences in each city.

Behind the music lies a network of distributors and operators who live and die by an unwritten code. The industry is described by the committee as "a gigantic conspiracy to extort millions of dollars through the use of force, threats of force, and economic persuasion."[3]

"The committee has found convincing evidence that organized criminal gangs are infiltrating into many legitimate businesses, including a large number of jukebox operating companies," Senator Kefauver reports to Congress. Speaking in his mellifluous Tennessee accent, the senator asserts that "there seems to be a natural affinity of underworld characters for the distribution of these machines."[4]

"The stakes are high," reporter Bob Greene writes, drawing on the committee's work in an investigation of the jukebox industry for *Newsday*. "In 1945 jukeboxes in Chicago alone swallowed nearly $15 million in nickels, dimes and quarters. Associations of jukebox operators are spreading throughout the country, forcing out or taking over small-time operators with the aid of ruthless and unscrupulous dealers."[5]

From the beginning, coin machine operators had a strong aversion to reporting an accurate count to the taxman. A cash business, jukeboxes offer a prime opportunity to launder money. One operator who seizes the opportunity is New York hoodlum Meyer Lansky. Known as the mob's banker, Lansky strategizes the transition of organized crime into legitimate enterprises. Lansky had run a profitable WurliTzer distributorship in South Florida in the 1930s. His salesmen could twist arms or break them.

Probing the relationship between the music machine industry and racketeers, Kefauver subpoenas Lansky to testify in New York. When the WurliTzer Co. faced weak sales in New York in the early 1940s, the company turned to Lansky to improve distribution. The announcement of his agreement to distribute WurliTzer jukeboxes in New York, New Jersey, and Connecticut in 1943 was celebrated with a photo in *Billboard*. The magazine quotes Wurlitzer executive Milton "Mike" Hammergren, who says, "We know that in Meyer Lansky we have a man who is liked and respected by everyone . . . we are confident that as Wurlitzer's new distributor in this territory he will make many new friends."[6]

With strong-arm sales techniques, Lansky's company takes over the New York/New Jersey market, and within two years, WurliTzer's machines dominate sales in the territory. A criminal visionary, Lansky becomes expert at washing millions of dollars in illegal income, then investing in legitimate enterprises, including hotels and spectacular casinos in Havana.

Called to testify before the Kefauver Committee, Lansky pleads the Fifth Amendment. He does this twice. Frustrated, the senator proposes a compromise. In return for his service to the United States in beating up Nazi spies working on the docks of New York during World War II, the committee will interrogate Lansky in a closed-door session, allowing the witness to avoid being cited for contempt and a possible prison term.

Granted the privacy of testifying to the Kefauver Committee out of sight of the television cameras, Lansky confirms his long relationship with WurliTzer. But the company grew sensitive to Lansky's notoriety and in 1947 asked him to sell his routes. "They said I was a bad risk for them," Lansky tells Senator Kefauver.[7]

Kefauver concludes that "there is now ample evidence that many juke box operating concerns are controlled by some of the country's most vicious criminal elements. They operate their juke box businesses in true gangster fashion, establishing mutually exclusive territories, falsifying records, and policing their jurisdictions by brute force."[8]

"Kefauver fever" sweeps the country. The senator announces a run for president in 1952. He defeats President Harry Truman in the New Hampshire Democratic primary and goes on to win 80 percent of the primaries. Concerned by the crime-busting senator's progressive views on civil rights and corporate responsibility, the backroom power brokers fix the convention, denying Kefauver the candidacy. Four years later, he is on the Democratic ticket as the candidate for vice president, in a losing cause.

THE EIGHT-YEAR GAP

The Fabulous Fifties. A house in the suburbs with a picket fence. *Father Knows Best*. Cars with tail fins. *I Like Ike*. Bomb shelters. Elvis.

Wolfe and Trudy fly up to his hometown in Canada. He lands in a farmer's field, leaving a trail of dust. Wolfe takes Trudy on a tour of his boyhood haunts: the family store, the pharmacy, the old swimming hole by the creek, the baseball field where he scored a home run and scored again with a Mennonite girl under the bleachers. He leaves out the last part.

Wolfe has flown with Trudy to Morden to attend the bris of Milton's infant son. A rabbi chants the Hebrew blessings, and a *moyle* makes the cut, a dramatic ritual to the gentile townsfolk who join the celebration of the arrival of a third generation of the Rabinovitch family. The boy is named David in memory of his grandfather, Wolfe and Milton's father Doc. Trudy loves the little blonde boy with big blue eyes. She's envious.

Back in their Chicago penthouse, Trudy, in slip and lingerie, removes her makeup, carefully inspecting her skin in the vanity mirror. She unclips her diamond earrings, stares at the sparkling stones in her hand, flings them like skipping stones across the glass surface.

At his dressing table, Wolfe looks up. Trudy reaches behind her neck, opens the clasp of her pearls. She turns and throws them across the room at Wolfe. What the ——?

Tears stream down her face. What good is all this? She wants stability and a family. And some part of Wolfe does too. In their forties, the biological clock has expired. If they can't have a baby, they can always adopt.

Wolfe takes out a mortgage to buy a house in Highland Park, a prestigious suburb of Chicago. As a child imagining the mythical uncle I had never met, I pictured a white stucco bungalow with a postage-stamp yard, like my other uncles' homes in the Winnipeg suburbs. Now I imagine Wolfe and Trudy lived in a house more compatible with the Craftsman, Prairie School, and International- Style homes of the area.

A serial entrepreneur, Wolfe succeeds with his vision for high fidelity in the home. His new company, the Continental Radio Corporation, rides the crest of middle-class consumerism. He's back in *Billboard*. He sends a unit for custom installation in the Prairie modern home my parents build in Morden. The radio has a brass grille with George Nelson–inspired numerals on the dial.

Wolfe's fertile mind spins forth new ideas. He designs and patents a machine for slaughtering and processing chickens. He tinkers in the lab, wiring up a burglar alarm system that is triggered by photoelectric cells. He builds a working prototype.

Then the trail of documentation goes cold. And something goes terribly wrong. Wolfe bottoms out.

We will next find him in Miami, drawn into a venture with high stakes. Up against powerful forces, Wolfe is caught between the Mob and the feds. The documents uncovered reveal in detail Wolfe's role in an epic caper—a story of money, guns, planes, gambling, and Wolfe's journey through the dark side of the American dream.

LIGHTNING IN A CATHODE RAY TUBE
Washington, D.C., 1958

In 1958, a new Senate investigation into organized crime begins to hold hearings. Officially the Select Committee on Improper Activities in Labor and Management, its member senators include rising star John F. Kennedy; future Republican presidential candidate Barry Goldwater; Sam Ervin, future chair of the Watergate hearings; and the committee chairman John McClellan, a crusty Democrat from Arkansas. Republican Senator Homer Capehart, who financed his political campaigns from a fortune made distributing jukeboxes for the WurliTzer Company, absents himself from most of the hearings.

Senator McClellan vows the committee will use its investigative and subpoena powers to reveal evidence of a mob-sponsored plot involving bribery, extortion, blackmail, and murder.

> *This current investigation will likely be one of the most important we have undertaken with references to the hoodlum effort to achieve legitimacy through association with unions and business enterprises. . . . In speaking of this industry we are prone to focus on jukeboxes, and there [sic] are, indeed, an integral part of the industry, with more than half a million currently in commercial operation today. . . . The stakes, therefore, in achieving control of this[the coin-operated machine] industry are very high indeed.*[9]

How did jukeboxes and the entire coin machine industry come under the control of the underworld? Senator McClellan:

> *First, the lucrative nature of the business itself; second, the fact that much of the business is conducted in cash and presents an excellent opportunity for the concealment and use of illicitly received revenues from other enterprises such as gambling, prostitution, and the sale of narcotics; and third, the very nature of the business which makes establishments in which these machines are most commonly placed subject to outside pressures.*[10]

The amount of money at play is staggering. Experts for the committee estimate the annual unreported income from coin machines at $2 billion in 1958, with another $300 to $400 million from jukeboxes. Adjusted for inflation, that would be more than $23 billion today.

McClellan has a righteous goal: to protect the "little guy" in a business where nickels add up to billions of dollars.

> *In attempting to achieve control over the industry, racketeers have found it necessary to insure what they like to call stability. But stability however, in their parlance, has come to mean monopoly. This stranglehold on the industry has been attempted through collusion between employers and associations with labor unions, some of which have been created for the sole purpose of acting as an enforcement area. The businessman who tries to oppose this combination frequently finds an organized drive started against the establishments with which he does business.*[11]

In many cities, the operators are members of the Teamsters Union, who picket or sabotage locations that refuse to take their jukeboxes. If a tavern tries to change jukeboxes, it might find its beer deliveries contaminated with urine. Or worse.

"During the development of this industry," investigator Arthur Kaplan testifies in 1958, "the operators discovered that the best ways to maximize their profits are to keep out other operators, to give minimal service to locations, to keep locations from changing operators so they don't have to keep moving machines, in other words, to restrain competition in their own favor."[12]

Like the Kefauver Committee eight years previously, McClellan's committee makes headlines with testimony that details the intimidation, money laundering, and industry complicity in organized crime's takeover of the coin machine industry. The star of the hearings is the young committee counsel Robert F. Kennedy, who conducts grueling interrogations of leading crime lords and their victims, exposing the methods and extent of criminal control of legitimate businesses.

Among the witnesses who face Kennedy under the hot television lights, Milton Hammergren represents the WurliTzer Company, the largest manufacturer of jukeboxes. In his memoir of the hearings, Kennedy notes that "Milton Hammergren set up the big gangsters in business: Meyer Lansky on the East Coast; Buster Wortman in St. Louis; 'Greasy Thumb' Guzik and Tony Accardo in Chicago."[13]

Kennedy: Were company officials upset about the use of force?

Hammergren: Company officials, of which I was one, yes, we didn't like it, but we still had to sell jukeboxes. We knew all about it, and we knew what the problems were. We tried to go along with it the best we could.

Kennedy: I mean if somebody, just in the course of trying to get your boxes distributed, if somebody was killed, that was taken as part of the trade?

Hammergren: That is one of the liabilities of the business, I would say.[14]

Kennedy: Looking back, was there a considerable amount of violence in connection with this industry?

Hammergren: Yes, there was violence, such as blowing out the windows of the store or blowing up an automobile or something of that nature, or beat a fellow up.

Kennedy: Is that part of the characteristics of the industry?

Hammergren: Yes; I would say so.

Kennedy: Were there also killings?

Hammergren: Yes, there was only one killing that I actually knew about.

Kennedy: Who was killed?

Hammergren: Lehme Kelly, a big operator, was shot one Sunday afternoon.

Kennedy: L-e-h-m-e Kelly, he was a big operator there?

Hammergren: Yes, sir; both ways. He weighed 540 pounds and he operated about 700 or 800 jukeboxes.

Kennedy: Why was he killed?

Hammergren: I don't know.[15]

Hammergren had succeeded Homer Capehart as head of sales for WurliTzer when Capehart went into politics. Despite his extensive experience in the coin machine industry, when Senator Capehart makes an appearance at the hearings, according to committee counsel Robert Kennedy, he "made no contribution. It seemed to me that in his questioning of a witness he almost invariably sided with those under investigation. It was most peculiar."[16]

Robert Kennedy will be appointed attorney general in 1961 following the election of his brother Senator John F. Kennedy as president. RFK will be assassinated in 1968 during his own run for the presidency.

While Kennedy conducts these interrogations on television, the largest money-laundering scheme in history secretly unfolds—with Wolfe Rabin at its center.

Chapter Five

Biggest Bank Robbery in the World

Chicago, June 1958

WOLFE DRIVES DOWN MICHIGAN AVENUE, DRAWING ON A MONTE Cristo. Pulls up at the Imperial Pawn Shop.

Wolfe pawns a pair of diamond earrings. He puts his hat on the counter while they negotiate. His once-thick head of hair has been reduced by pattern baldness to dark rims around the sides.

The pawnbroker counts out six $20 bills. They cost ten times as much; Wolfe protests, to no avail. He's already burned through the $2,500 he borrowed from his brother Leon. He removes the gold Masonic ring from his pinky, considers pawning it, slips it back. He stubs out his cigarette in the ashtray, takes the cash for the earrings and the pawn ticket. Back in a week, he assures the pawnbroker. He replaces his hat on his head, shrugs his shoulders on the way out the door.

New Kensington, Pennsylvania, June 21, 1958

A government-issue Ford sedan pulls up at the entrance to the Church of Mount St. Peter, an impressive edifice distinguished by its Michigan red sandstone. A red-haired man in his thirties alights, mounts the grand stairs to the church.

In the rectory across the courtyard, the curtain draws open across a third-floor window, revealing Sam Mannarino, who had been Wolfe's partner in the jukebox business. Watching.

When the man raps at the massive doors, a priest in a cassock appears. The man reaches into his breast pocket, takes out his wallet, flashes a badge. Agent Thomas Forsyth, FBI.

Father Nicola Fusco, white-haired, heavy-set, has been the pastor for New Kensington's 10,000 Italian Catholics for more than thirty years. He knows everything. But he doesn't know this FBI agent. Not of the faith.

The priest welcomes him to the church. In the main vestibule, he points out the overscale bronze sculpture of the crucifix.

"Viewed from His right side," he tells the agent in his Italian lilt, "Our Savior gives evidence of a most painful agony. Viewed from His left side, He smiles. It is indeed very singular."

Agent Forsyth asks Father Fusco if he has seen Sam Mannarino.

"Why do you want to know?" the priest retorts.

Forsyth holds up an envelope. There's an outstanding subpoena. From a federal grand jury.

Father Fusco is furious.

"I'm a pure-blooded Sicilian. The Mannarinos are my boys. The government is persecuting them for things that are quite legal in Italy!"

The FBI man backs off, through the church, out the doors. Which are still being watched from the third-floor window by Sam Mannarino, who breathes a sigh of relief.[1]

MONDO CONDO
Miami, 1958

By the mid-1950s, expanded airline routes and improved air conditioning attract northerners who become seasonal residents to Florida. Television antennas sprout on the rooftops. The mob lives in its own mondo condo. The families of the *famiglia* from New York, Philadelphia, Pittsburgh, Cleveland, and Detroit inhabit entire apartment complexes from Palm Beach to the Keys.

Twilight encroaches as Wolfe's rented convertible approaches the security gate of the Biltmore Terrace hotel.[2] Wolfe Rabin for Mr. Rothman. The guard recognizes Wolfe, waves him through.

An FBI report notes that "the Biltmore Terrace Hotel, although to all outward appearances a first-class hotel, is frequented by a number of

Cubans who are anti-Fidel Castro, and the hotel has the reputation of being a hot bed for Cuban revolutionary activities. The hotel is allegedly owned by ex-associates of [former Cuban president] Batista and Norman Rothman."[3]

Wolfe steps through the elevator doors into the tenth-floor penthouse. He is greeted by a heavily made-up, forty-ish brunette dripping with jewels, who offers her cheek. He gives her a peck.

"So good to see you, Ethel."

But she is shrewish.

"I'll take you to his lordship."

She motions Wolfe through the penthouse to the patio by the pool. A broad-shouldered, dripping wet man climbs out of the water. Norman Rothman, forty-three, aka "Roughhouse" and "the Capper."[4] A *shtarker*.[5] He shrugs on a robe, welcomes Wolfe.

Men like Rothman are accorded special status by the Mafia. They call them half-assed wise guys, Jews who can be trusted to do business. But they can never get "made," can never be "family." La Cosa Nostra's blood oath is for Italian Catholics only. According to an FBI report, "Rothman, in his position with Kelly and Sammy Mannarino, members of 'the Outfit' in Pittsburgh, is in a position to furnish information to the 'right people' who could cause people to be 'rubbed out.'"[6]

A scrawny young man comes out of the pool. Rothman flicks a towel at him, a little harder than playful.

"That's my son Cappy," he introduces Wolfe. "He's going to med school."[7]

Rothman owns a piece of the Tropicana, a landmark casino in Havana. His silent partner is the dictator Colonel Fulgencio Batista. The Cuban strongman's personal skim is in the millions—dollars, not pesos. In another deal, with Batista's brother-in-law, Rothman operates all the slot machines outside Havana. The wages of sin aren't subject to tax.

But rebels are gathering in the mountains in Cuba, rallying behind a charismatic schoolteacher, Fidel Castro. The 26th of July Movement's objectives are distribution of land to peasants, nationalization of public services, industrialization, honest elections, and large-scale education reform.

They are communists opposed to gambling as exploitation of the masses. The revolution does not bode well for the casino business. The Capper says they should take out Castro. Wolfe objects.

> Wolfe: Castro is going to want his skim just like all the other tin pot dictators. If he takes over, you'll want to have him in your pocket.
>
> Rothman: So, smart guy?
>
> Wolfe: Keep your friends close. Keep your enemies closer. Batista. Castro. They're both greedy bastards.
>
> Rothman: Come to Havana. Bring your wife. Be my guests at the Tropicana.

Havana, 1958

Havana. City of rumba, samba, mambo, conga lines, rum, Eartha Kitt, Nat King Cole, Frank Sinatra, Errol Flynn, Papa Hemingway. With a crackdown on gambling in the United States and a Senate committee investigating organized crime, Cuba is an island of opportunity, a naughty playground beyond the reach of the Internal Revenue Service.

Wolfe and Trudy arrive at the Tropicana, considered the most beautiful nightclub in the world. Card tables lit by crystal chandeliers are packed with vacationing Americans in Rothman's fiefdom, the gambling room or "carpet shop" just off the main lobby. Crowds jostle at the roulette wheels and craps tables. Compulsive players feed coins into the one-arm bandits, the slot machines lining the walls.

You have to go through the casino to get to the dining, dancing, and entertainment. Palm trees rise over the tables and through the roof in the "Paradise under the Stars," where the exotic dancer Olga Chaviano headlines a steamy floor show with a sequined chorus line dancing on catwalks among the palms.

After the show, Wolfe takes Trudy backstage. The voluptuous star disrobes, un-self-consciously shedding her costume. If Trudy is a Jewish guy's *shiksa* dream, then Norman Rothman has scored the

Figure 5.1. Wolfe Rabin in Havana, Cuba, 1949. Still frame from 16 mm Koda-chrome, shot by Trudy Rabin. COPYRIGHT THE AUTHOR.

ultimate Latina trophy wife, Olga Chaviano, thirty-three, a rumba dancer, singer, entertainer, and Cuban movie star.

An olive-skinned toddler runs up, tugs at Wolfe's trousers. Wolfe sweeps the boy up in his arms. What he and Trudy always wanted. But it never happened.

Wolfe hands the child back to his mother.

Wolfe: Faustino Rothman? That's an unusual name.

Olga: My deal with *el diablo.*

At the craps table, Trudy blows on the dice for luck. Wolfe rolls. He rakes the chips across the green felt. He is back in the game. He hands Trudy a roll of silver pesos to play the slots.

Sam Mannarino saunters into the bar. Although the jukebox company had blown up in the courts over patent rights, he greets

Figure 5.2. Gertrude "Trudy" Rabin in Havana, 1949. Still frame from Wolfe Rabin home movie. COPY-RIGHT THE AUTHOR.

Wolfe with a warm handshake and a clap on the shoulder.

Expanding their investments from the coin machine rackets, Mannarino and his brother Kelly had bought the gambling concession at the Sans Souci, Havana's oldest nightclub, a tropical fantasy in the style of a Spanish colonial villa seven miles outside Havana. But when Batista assumed power in 1953, he forced out the Mannarinos.

In 1957, the dictator's brother-in-law, in his capacity as minister of sport, made a deal with Mannarino and Rothman for the gambling rights in the territory outside Havana. They installed more than two thousand slot machines. But by the summer of 1958, the slots were losing money due to breakage and Batista's skim of 50 percent off the top,[8] an operation yielding between $5 million and $10 million a year.[9]

Rothman proposes a scheme to get the Pittsburgh racketeer back in the business of gambling in Cuba. To pull it off, they need three things.

Wolfe ticks them off on his fingers: "Money. Banks have money. Guns. The Army has guns. Shipping. We need an air force."

Rothman says he will talk to some pilots who hang out at his bar.

Mannarino: You know a guy could handle the finances?

Wolfe opens his palms, shrugs.

Wolfe: Don't I owe you?

Rothman: You see, Sammy? Your guys can handle the rough stuff. But this kind of thing, it takes a *Yiddische kopf.*[10] (He stage winks at Wolfe.)

They are about to launch a complex plot. No one, not even the key participants, will ever see the whole picture. Fragments come into focus, but the jagged edges don't necessarily fit. Events play out in parallel. The biggest money-laundering scheme in history will begin in Montreal with what appears to be an isolated robbery.

BONDS
Montreal, April 23, 1958
A red neon sign for *Fournitures de Soudage/Welding Supplies* hangs in the darkened window of a shop on Rue Parthenais. At 2:00 a.m., the street is quiet, only the occasional passing car in the late spring snow. Around the alley in the back, a panel van backs up to the loading dock.

Two men in balaclavas carry items through the door to a third who loads them into the van. They heft large cylinders marked "oxygen," another stenciled "acetylene," electric drills, hosing for welding and cutting, an armful of army surplus respirators and kit bags.

Alarms are ringing. Sirens echo in the distance. The men climb aboard as the van lurches forward into the snowy night.

Brockville, Ontario, May 5, 1958
Police tapes cordon off a four-story stone building in the historic town halfway between Montreal and Toronto. Church bells peal in the distance. Black and whites block the street. Detectives push their way through the milling throng, up the steps, through the double doors, into the vestibule. Through a second set of doors, where they are struck by the acrid odor of charred wood and paper. Traces of smoke hang in the air.

A fireman leads the detectives into the main lobby of the Brockville Trust and Savings Bank, facing the wickets at the savings department counter. Behind the counter, rows of accounting desks. Offices for the bank manager, mortgages and loans, estates and trusts. Next to the great vault, five thicknesses of brick mortared together encasing half-inch steel plate. Where millions of dollars in stocks, bonds, cash, and jewelry are placed for safekeeping. The sole entry to the vault is through an imposing ten-foot-high steel door that is set on a timer but not alarmed.

Immediately to the left of the vault is a wooden door opening inward. Opening the door lets out smoke and dust. Through the door to a landing covered in rubble of bricks, plaster, mortar, and badly charred shelves. Strewn about are a large number of documents and Canada savings bonds in denominations from $100 to $10,000. The brick wall has been blasted through, leaving a jagged hole nearly two feet in diameter. The hole leads into the vault.

A cord plugged in on the wall leads to a large electric fan inside the vault, slowly turning. The doors of three large safes swing ajar. Two have been cut through, and the combination lock has been knocked off the

Figure 5.3. The rubble at the Brockville Trust, 1958. Thieves blasted through five feet of brick and steel, May 3, 1958, to enter the vault at Brockville Trust in "the biggest bank robbery in the world."
ONTARIO PROVINCIAL POLICE PHOTO DISTRIBUTED BY CP WIRE SERVICE.

third. The doors from dozens of safety deposit boxes litter the floor. Police boots slosh through water on the floor, littered with charred papers and bonds of various issuers and denominations.

Tools have been left behind in a hurry—crowbars, picks, drills, metal cylinders of oxygen and acetylene, respirators, and kit bags. A dirty trail on the floor from the door to the landing leads to a washroom in the department of trusts and estates. More bonds lie scattered amid the damp and the dust.

The old-fashioned tin ceiling in the estates and trusts department has a hole big enough for a man to get through. A ten-foot steel ladder leans up into the hole.

Police boots and blue serge trousers mount the ladder through the hole in the ceiling into an office on the second floor. The desks and office furniture have been pushed back to the walls, and the inlaid linoleum has been torn up. The lettering on the pebbled glass door reads "A. A. Crawley, Chartered . . . ," but the part that used to read "Accountants" has been smashed.

Through the unlocked door to a hallway. A woman's scarf on the floor. A raincoat on the landing. Stairs leading down two flights to the basement beneath the Brockville Trust and Savings. Past the electrical panels, the switchboard, the washrooms to a window looking into a window well five feet deep. The steel mesh that had covered the window is on the floor along with a padlock cut in two. An iron grill covers the window well from the street above, where a whole cavalry of police and a large crowd are now on the scene.[11]

$2,240,000 STOLEN IN BANK IN CANADA; Vault in Brockville Cracked—Negotiable Paper Taken—Suspect is Seized

Special to the New York Times, *May 06, 1958, MONTREAL, May 5—Proficient cracksmen broke into a vault of the Brockville Trust and Savings Company, about halfway between here and Toronto, over the weekend and made off with paper of uncertain value.[12]*

BANK LOOT TOTAL RISES; Canadian Safecrackers' Haul $10,000,000

BROCKVILLE, Ont., May 7 (AP)—The loot in the week-end safecracking at the Brockville Trust Company was estimated today to total as much as $10,000,000.[13]

Calculating for inflation, in 2022, the value of the bonds stolen from Brockville Trust would equal approximately $500 million.

Canadian newspapers headline the story "the crime of the century." The FBI calls it "the biggest bank robbery in the world."[14] The Brockville police chief charges that the heist was the work of a highly organized group of criminals. The job was done expertly, rapidly, and methodically. The Ontario attorney general suspects a slick international organization, anonymous masterminds who hired a crew of specialists.[15]

Montreal, May 6, 1958

A clue emerges from the rubble at the Brockville Trust, a passbook for a bank account registered to Jean-Guy Rondeau of Montreal.

Rondeau, twenty-three, a tough blonde French Canadian, drives through Outremont, his working-class neighborhood. Red and blue lights flash in the rearview mirror. Thinks about flooring it, but there's a cop car in front. And another alongside. They force him to a screeching halt at the curb.

Guns drawn, the police order him out of the car. They slam him against the car, rough him up, cuff him. Hands tear through his pockets. ID, smokes, coins, billfold, and a small key with a tag.

The key fits a locker at Montreal's *Gare Centrale* (Central Station). In it, detectives find a brown army kit bag and a blue zippered satchel stuffed with bonds and stock and share certificates. Cameras flash on the cops displaying the evidence. Tearing apart Rondeau's apartment yields another stash. The total recovered comes to more than $1.2 million. The serial numbers on the bonds coincide with those on the Brockville Trust's list of missing securities.

Rondeau keeps his mouth shut, saying he is "not in a position to be cooperative." In his dank cell at Bordeaux Prison, he is not in a position to do much of anything. The young French Canadian is merely a foot soldier, unaware of the grand scheme to be financed with bonds from Brockville.

MANNARINO MOB FLIES HIGH

Western Pennsylvania's biggest gambling operation is luring those who live by their luck to New Kensington. The $2 million-a-year craps and barbout (dice) layout is run by the Mannarino mob.

This little Las Vegas, a gambling house the jack from numbers built, is on the second floor of Triangle Billiards. Immune from local police interference, it caters brazenly to the traveling gambler—the man who'll drive miles to risk his money. It is operated by Kelly and his brother Sam Mannarino, an aging hoodlum who a few years ago almost lost his silk shirt in a casino at the Sans Souci in Havana. — Pittsburgh Post-Gazette, May 23, 1958[16]

Elk County, Pennsylvania

Sam Mannarino is not a suspect in the Brockville bonds robbery. But an all-points bulletin is out for him. Police and state troopers are on a manhunt in western Pennsylvania. A well-known sportsman, Sam disappears into the woods and is reported missing from a hunting expedition.

As the dawn breaks, Mannarino trudges up a trail, a burly figure in canvas hunting jacket, rifle slung over his shoulder. He stumbles into a clearing by a gravel service road leading to a pumping station. It has a pay phone, and Sam has a nickel. The state patrol soon arrives to rescue him, to his chagrin.

Sam Made Woods Turn Too Short!
New Kensington's Mannarino Finally Emerges From Forest

Reporting the incident, the Pittsburgh *Post-Gazette* notes, "Sam was not hiding from the law. Another member of the Mannarino family, Sam's brother Gabriel, known as 'Kelly,' disappeared last fall. But he was turned up by New York State Police as a delegate to an international gangland convention."[17]

Kelly had worked his way up to capo for John LaRocca, the boss of Pittsburgh's Sicilian Mafia. He attended the infamous Mob summit at Apalachin, New York, in 1957. Fleeing the feds when they surrounded the upstate hideaway, he stumbled in the woods and was detained by the FBI. The Department of Justice later attempted to serve Kelly with a subpoena on charges of conspiring to obstruct justice by lying about the nature of the underworld meeting, but he couldn't be found.

New York City, June 24, 1958

Wolfe drinks with Sam Mannarino at the Café Montmartre, a Manhattan supper club. "Where are we going to get the money," he wants to know. Mannarino chomps on his cigar. The answer could be coming our way. He indicates a stocky, balding man who has stopped for a few words at another table.

Mannarino greets Giuseppe "Pep" Cotroni, thirty-eight, head of the "largest and most notorious narcotic syndicate on the North American continent," according to his file in the U.S. Bureau of Narcotics Investigation (BNI). Born in Reggio Calabria on the Italian boot, Cotroni grew up on the ruthless streets of Montreal's Little Italy. His rap sheet includes convictions for theft and receiving, theft by breaking into, theft with violence, and possession of stolen bonds. The BNI file describes Cotroni as "a supplier of major Mafia traffickers in the United States with direct French-Corsican sources of supply. A terrorist and a vicious hoodlum."[18]

Pep Cotroni and his brother Vicenzo, aka "Vic the Egg," control organized crime in Montreal. Cotroni had survived a rival racketeer's attempt to assassinate him by poisoning his wine. He represented the Montreal branch of La Cosa Nostra at the organized crime summit at Apalachin in 1957. When the feds closed in, he escaped through the woods over the border to Canada.

Cotroni asks if they heard about the blast at the bank in Brockville. "Yeah, all over the papers." He shrugs. "Didn't have nothin' to do with it." But he might have access to those bonds.

Mannarino: What do we want with bonds? We need cash.

Investors consider bonds to be the safest form of debt security, but they aren't commonly used in underworld transactions. Bonds are issued by all levels of government and corporations to raise financing. Registered bonds bear the name of the owner, which is on record with the issuer.

But the bonds Cotroni has are bearer bonds. They have no individual's name and are readily negotiable. These bonds can be passed around from owner to owner, and when a person receives one, it does not require endorsement. No signature necessary. Just like a dollar bill. Possession is proof of ownership.

Mannarino asks if Cotroni needs a broker to trade the bonds. Wolfe has been silent throughout. Mannarino introduces him as "a friend of ours" with experience in handling international finances.

Montreal, July 28, 1958

A figure in a raincoat passes through the massive Corinthian columns of the main branch of the Bank of Commerce on Rue Saint-Jacques. René Savard, thirty-one, enters the central hall of the bank, lights a cigarette, looks around.

He walks up to the securities window at the far end of the hall. Conducting the transaction in French, he slides a series of Government of Canada bonds, $6,000 in total, through the brass window. The starchy Anglophone securities trader scratches a list of the series numbers with a fountain pen. He takes the bonds to the trading desk. Savard smokes, fidgets, waiting.

When the trader returns, he explains to Savard that the bonds are unissued. They have no name on them, and the date of issue is not filled in. They do not have a rubber stamp from an issuing financial institution.

Alarm bells ring throughout the bank. Savard turns, facing a phalanx of police, their guns drawn and pointed at him.

Savard is arrested, but the police have no evidence to link him to the bank blast in Brockville. The best they can do is charge him with possession of stolen bonds. Savard walks free on bail with cash sent by Pep Cotroni.

Chicago, September 10, 1958

A dark-haired, olive-skinned man in a tan suit enters the brass doors of an art deco tower on the Miracle Mile. He scans the building directory, enters the elevator, asks the operator for the eleventh floor. Down the hallway, he stops at a pebbled glass door lettered "William W. Rabin, Consultant."

Alfredo Garcia is an agent for the 26th of July Movement, the group led by Fidel Castro who have set out to overthrow Fulgencio Batista, the president/dictator of Cuba. Wolfe ushers him into his office.

Garcia indicates that Wolfe should draw the blinds. He clicks on a desk light. Garcia offers Wolfe a Monte Cristo, proffers his lighter.

"We would like to engage your services to facilitate some international money transactions," he tells Wolfe, speaking precisely chosen words with a Cuban accent.

Wolfe blows smoke from his cigar, sets it on the ashtray, leans forward.

"We have a substantial amount of bonds," Garcia continues, "which need to be delivered to our associates in Europe."

Wolfe: What sum are you talking?

Garcia: Two or three million dollars. For the first tranche.

Wolfe: What's in it for me?

Garcia: $5,000 up front. For your expenses. And $250,000 in bonds.

Wolfe is intrigued. This could be the big score he needs.

Months later, when the FBI begins investigating the money, they can find no evidence of Wolfe's office. No listing on the building directory. The elevator man doesn't recognize his photo. Agent Robert Malone gets a queasy feeling. The only connection the FBI agent finds is Wolfe's mail drop in the lobby.

Over the Great Lakes, September 10, 1958

Wolfe rides shotgun in a single-engine Cessna, cruising over Lake Michigan, compass bearing north by northeast. The pilot is Kent Tomlinson, forty-six, tall and gawky. In a story cast with assorted shysters and ruthless racketeers, Kent is perhaps Wolfe's most unlikely accomplice.

But Tomlinson has a certain charisma, of the all-American country boy variety.

A dance instructor, Fuller Brush salesman, and all-around bunco artist, Kent Tomlinson struck it rich in the 1940s when he invented the rubber chicken plucking finger, a device to pluck chicken feathers in poultry plants. He flies the Cessna to promote the plucker and survey his expanding chain of poultry plants.

Back in 1949, Wolfe had approached Tomlinson with his own invention, an apparatus for stunning and killing poultry on an assembly-line basis. Kent had licensed the patent, and the two kept in touch. When Wolfe called him to fly up to Canada for a few days fishing, he said sure.

Kent: Do you believe in ufo's?

Wolfe: You mean, like flying saucers?

Kent: I've seen them. And the *grays*. The extra-terrestrials they bring here.

Wolfe: You're kidding me!

Kent: They are totally hairless, no ears, no nose, no mouth—just a slit—a very narrow pointed chin, large eyes.[19]

Wolfe rolls his eyes.

The Cessna flies across the world's longest undefended border into Canada. Landing at Montreal airfield, they present their driver's licenses to the Canadian immigration officer. Just flew up for some fishing. The officer waves them through. No passports required.

Montreal, September 10, 1958

Wolfe and Kent check into the Mount Royal, a grand railroad hotel. The clerk hands Wolfe a message.

In his room, Wolfe looks through the Montreal phone book. Circles a name. Tears out the page.

There is a knock from the door to the adjoining suite. Room service? Wolfe opens the door, revealing Sam Mannarino.

In a booth at Cotroni's Spaghetti House, the head of the Montreal clan pours from a bottle of Valpolicella. With napkins tied around their necks, Wolfe and Mannarino enjoy lobster and pasta.

Cotroni is upset with the French Canadians, Rondeau for getting caught with the bonds and Savard for attempting to exchange the bonds at the bank, too eager to cash in on his share. *Maudits Christ*, even a dog knows not to shit in its own backyard.

Cotroni needs to unload the bonds and convert them to cash. Mannarino offers him a deal. He will take bearer bonds only, no registered bonds. Large denominations only. He offers ten cents on the dollar face value, in cash. If the bonds can be sold for their face value, there is a fortune to be made.

After a night of intense negotiation, they settle at twenty-one cents on the dollar. It will take time to sort the deliverables, $100,000 in Canadian bonds. Wolfe will be trusted with the transfer.

Back at the English bar at the Mount Royal, where corporate titans discuss high finance, Wolfe confers over Crown Royal with Kent Tomlinson. Wolfe and his pal are joined by the gunrunner/pilot Joe Merola, who has been sent from Miami by Norman Rothman. Merola's FBI file describes him as "a notorious smuggler, gunrunner and general no-goodnik."[20] The CIA calls him "a fast dealer with connections at all levels in many foreign countries. . . . His information is usually very good."[21]

Merola boasts about his relationship with the Mannarinos. "One time, Sam's brother Kelly took me to New York City with him and he introduced me to Vito Genovese. He told them he was making me into a don."

Glasses of Crown Royal are refilled. Merola continues:

Another occasion, Kelly gave me a package and told me to deliver it to New York City without opening it. And when I had delivered the package and it was opened, it was found to contain only cut up newspaper. They had a good laugh on me. They put me to other tests, they had me arrested by the cops in New Kensington. All of which were designed to test me to see if I could be trusted and would remain silent.[22]

Next morning Wolfe, posh in camel-colored cashmere coat, walks up St. Catherines to the Hudson's Bay Company department store. In the men's furnishings, he looks over attaché cases, briefcases, settles on a brown leather satchel with straps and locking clasps. He pays cash for the briefcase. On his way out of the store, he passes the perfume counter, catches himself, returns to the counter, where he flirts with an attractive French Canadian saleswoman, selects a bottle of Chanel No. 5, and purchases it from her.

September 11, 1958
The Cessna is hosed to the fuel pump at Windsor, Ontario, airfield. A U.S. Customs agent inspects the plane.

Agent: Purpose of the trip?
Wolfe: [pats his satchel] Business.
Agent: Anything to declare?

Wolfe takes out two bottles of Crown Royal and the Chanel No. 5 he bought for Trudy. The customs agent notices the Masonic ring on Wolfe's pinkie.

Agent: Okay, brother. That's duty free. You're clear to go.

With Kent at the controls, the Cessna taxis down the runway and lifts off across the Detroit River, on a vector toward Chicago.

Chicago, September 16, 1958
Wolfe drives to the Central National Bank, an art deco building at the corner of Roosevelt and Halsted. His new briefcase in hand, he arranges to rent a large safety deposit box. He signs the ledger with a flourish. "William W. Rabin."

Clerk: What does the "W" stand for?
Wolfe: It's just an initial. Like the President. Harry S Truman.

The clerk gives him two small keys and escorts Wolfe to the vault. They enter through the heavy steel door, unlock and remove a metal drawer from the safety deposit box. Satchel in hand, Wolfe wraps an arm around the box and takes it to a private room.

He removes bundles of bonds from the satchel, neatly stacking them into the box. In the intimacy of the four walls, he savors the moment, alone with enough money for him and Trudy to vanish forever on a tropical island paradise.

When he emerges, the clerk accompanies him to the vault, where they place the box back in its slot and lock it with two keys.

The clerk points Wolfe to the bank's commercial loan office. The vice president, Frank Pepe, forty-five, greets Wolfe as a long-standing client.

Wolfe opens the clasps on the satchel, removes a handful of bonds, drops them on the desk.

Pepe: Where did you get all these bonds?
Wolfe: They're from my mother's estate.

Inspecting the documents, Pepe sees they are Dominion of Canada bonds, wartime Victory Bonds, in large denominations. He remembers that Wolfe is from Canada. Makes sense.

Pepe: What will you do with the loan?
Wolfe: I'm reorganizing my company.

Ordinarily, the banker explains, if they were U.S. Treasury bonds, the bank would loan up to 95 percent of the face value; since these are foreign bonds, the bank's rate is seventy cents on the dollar. Best he can do. Since Wolfe is known to the bank, they have ample security.

The bank executive writes a loan to Wolfe for $10,000 against the Canadian bonds. The bonds are sent to the collateral teller, who returns with a receipt. Wolfe requests a cashier's check for $2,500 made out to his brother Leon, another to himself for the balance.

Heady with the successful bonds trade, he meets Kent outside the bank. His friend is in a squeeze, behind on his payments to a steel company that is fabricating an ice machine he is promoting. Wolfe has signed a line of credit for $30,000, but it is overdrawn. He needs to get Kent off the hook.

They drive to the steel company office. Wolfe reaches into his pocket, flashes a fat roll, drops a pile of $1,000 bills on the counter. Flush for the first time in years, he can't control himself.

Wolfe: You want to know how to make a million? It's easy!

For a smart guy, how could he have such hubris?

Montreal, September 19, 1958
Wolfe arrives in Montreal on Trans Canada Airlines. At the immigration desk, he tells the officer he has come to visit his sister. A limousine driver holds a sign with Wolfe's name. The chauffeur is Cotroni's man René Savard, awaiting trial for possession of stolen bonds. He drives Wolfe through the cobbled streets of Old Montreal.

Wolfe meets with Pep Cotroni in his import/export office over the restaurant. From across the street, a long lens is trained on the second-floor window. Cotroni is under surveillance by the Royal Canadian Mounted Police (RCMP), who suspects that packets of narcotics are hidden in pasta shipments from Italy.

Wolfe has working capital from the bank loan he negotiated in Chicago. He plans to leverage it with more bonds. He negotiates a deal with Cotroni for the bonds: half up front, half in thirty days. He flies back to Chicago confident that he will be able to pay Cotroni with cash from selling the bonds.

DAY OF ATONEMENT
Chicago, September 23, 1958
It is *erev* Yom Kippur, the beginning of the Day of Atonement. On the holiest night of the year for Jews, Temple Beth Israel is packed, men in their finest suits, women in a fashion parade of outrageous hats. Wolfe, Leon, and Val attend the service, a ritual, tradition, an occasion to honor their parents. The modern Reform temple with its stained-glass windows and urban middle-class congregants is a world away from the tiny

Orthodox synagogue over Steinkopf's store in Morden, where Wolfe and Leon had been raised.

The congregation rises at the call to prayer. The cantor chants the haunting melody of the Kol Nidre, the prayer to rescind all vows. In the Jewish faith, it is considered the opportunity to make right all wrongs done to others.

Wolfe feels a tug on his shoulder, turns to the man next to him, Sam Mannarino, in skullcap and prayer shawl. Mannarino wipes a tear from his eye. It's beautiful, he says, like opera. It chokes me up. He hands Wolfe a thick envelope. Wolfe smoothly tucks it into the breast pocket of his suit.

Further along the pew, Leon's wife Val looks on, disapprovingly.

Chicago, September 25, 1958

Commuting to Montreal carrying small quantities of bonds is growing riskier. Wolfe ponders how to make a substantial trade. He needs to go somewhere the banks are capable of handling large sums with absolute discretion. Somewhere beyond the reach of the Internal Revenue Service.

With his sidekick Tomlinson, Wolfe goes to the Chicago Board of Trade building, to the office of the Corydon Travel Agency. Appraising Wolfe's tailored suit, gold watch, and expensive satchel, manager George Hoyt, forty-nine, senses a big spender.

Wolfe introduces himself as a consultant with a large international consortium. They have come to plan a trip to Europe. He would like to go to Zürich, Luxembourg, and Monaco. First class.

Kent asks if the travel agent knows of any airline pilots who might be interested in flying for the Cuban Revolutionary Armed Forces. The agent is taken aback by the inquiry. Wolfe abruptly changes the subject, glancing daggers at Tomlinson. Not the sharpest knife in the drawer.

He inquires if they have foreign currency for sale. If they have Swiss francs, he will take them off their hands. He prefers to travel with cash. Better than traveler's checks.

The travel agent explains that he will need payment in advance; being first class, the tickets are several thousand dollars. Wolfe assures him that they are dealing in large funds and can take care of all their obligations. He reaches down into his satchel.

Wolfe: This is full of bonds I need to clip. The money is no problem.

He tells the agent to prepare an itinerary, call when it is ready.

Montreal, September 27, 1958

Kent Tomlinson's Cessna makes the journey across the Great Lakes, again. Kent goes on a rant about a remote section of desert in Nevada called Area 51. That's where the aliens land.

Loony, Wolfe thinks. But entertaining. Reminds him of the Jules Verne novels he read when he was a kid.

Wolfe is in Montreal so frequently that the Mount Royal holds the same room for him. The room service cart contains the remains of lunch. Wolfe stubs out a cigarette. Holed up waiting for word from Cotroni, he takes out the page torn from the phone book, lifts the handset, asks the hotel operator to place the call.

His sister Ruby answers, surprised to hear his voice. Ruby, two years older than Wolfe, had been the betrayed in a family love triangle. Their younger sister Beryl, the blonde Bette Davis look-alike, had a romance with Ruby's husband. *Who could blame him? It was Beryl.* Ruby's marriage was shattered, leaving her to raise two boys without support. Because divorce in Catholic Quebec was not permitted, the dissolution of her marriage had taken an Act of Parliament.[23]

Wolfe takes Ruby and her teenage son to dinner at the Beaver Club, an Anglo bastion in the French Canadian city. Another world from the vice and violence of Pep Cotroni's Montreal. He loves the role of the generous uncle and being able to let down his guard with family. He entertains them with stories of his celebrity acquaintances like Bing Crosby and Hank Greenberg.

Brooklyn, New York, September 26, 1958

A gun dealer-informant reports to the FBI that a leader of the Cuban Revolutionary Council wants to meet with a Mafioso named "Big Joe" Merola. The informant meets with Merola and two Cubans in an apartment on Riverside Drive. Merola tells the dealer that he is interested in purchasing large quantities of firearms including machine guns, automatic rifles, bazookas, carbines, and grenades. Merola claims he supplied more than a million dollars' worth of arms during the Cuban rebellion and that he and his associates anticipate extensive gambling concessions in Cuba from the new government.

On the basis of this information, the Alcohol and Tobacco Tax Division temporarily loans the informant a number of confiscated weapons in order that he will have representative stock to show Merola.

New York City, September 28, 1958

An Edsel station wagon arrives at the Warwick Hotel. The man in the passenger seat rolls down his window, waves to a stocky, swarthy man approaching—Joe Merola.

Raising the tailgate, the men give Merola a large rectangular case. He carries it through the lobby and up to his room, where he opens it on the bed to reveal a .45-caliber Thompson machine gun.

Later, in the bar, he returns the case to the delivery men.

"This is what I want. Get me all you can. But clean them up."[24]

Chicago, September 29, 1958

Wolfe is running on adrenaline. From Montreal to Chicago directly to the bank, where he exchanges more bonds. The clerk types cashier's checks for $100,000.

Wolfe operates from an office at the Rek Chemical Company, a Mannarino front run out of a warehouse. He fumbles through the desk drawer for a pair of scissors.

Bearer bonds have coupons printed along the side of the certificate, one for each scheduled interest payment over the life of the bond. A bond with a face value of $1,000 and a coupon rate of 5 percent will pay total coupons of $50 per year. On the due date, the owner must detach the coupon and present it for payment.

Wolfe goes to work with the scissors.

Leon enters without knocking. Startled, Wolfe covers up, but Leon sees the bonds on the desk and the coupons Wolfe has clipped. Wolfe has kept his brother in the dark about his activities, to protect him. He motions to Leon to shut the door.

Wolfe confesses that he is in a jam. He owes Mannarino the advance for the first tranche of bonds, he owes Cotroni for the bonds on consignment, and now he owes the bank for the loans against the bonds. But he's got a plan. A way out. He will come out rich. He takes a bottle of scotch from a desk drawer, pours two tumblers. They drink. *L'chaim.* Leon has seen it all before. With Wolfe, you've got to shoot the moon and hold tight for the ride.

At Central National Bank, the clerk types cashier's checks, the first being payable to the order of Kent Industries in the amount of $2,000; the next being payable to the order of Kent Tomlinson Company, in the amount of $1,790; the third check being payable to the order of Kent Industries in the amount of $3,746.04 ; the next item being payable to the order of Kent Industries, Inc., in the amount of $5,000; and three checks to William W. Rabin totaling $75,000.[25]

Wolfe is trading so many bonds that the loan officer suggests he get a broker's license. Wolfe considers. Not a bad idea.

He returns to the travel agency, where he counts more thousand-dollar bills from his money clip, accepts the tickets in a portfolio. He asks directions to the nearest passport photographer.

CHAPTER SIX

Dollye

EUROPE

Frankfurt, October 6, 1958

WOLFE LOOKS OUT THE WINDOW, SEES THE SNOW ENCRUSTED ALPS below. First class on a TWA Starliner in the golden age of air travel is a luxury Wolfe enjoys. He turns to his seat mate, an attractive brunette in her twenties with a certain glow about her. Dollye Tomlinson, twenty-seven, is Kent Tomlinson's wife and a former beauty queen.

"Did y'all tell your wife I was traveling with you?" She speaks in a soft South Texas drawl.

"Are you kidding?" Wolfe responds, image of an angry Trudy appears in his mind. "She'd blow a gasket."

"Kent's going to meet us in Paris. And the two of you are in business together." She's matter of fact. Then a flirtatious look crosses her face. "A powerful man needs to have an attractive woman at his side," she says. "Makes a strong impression."

Wolfe asks her how she got together with Kent, who is closer to Wolfe's age.

"It was the Fourth of July at the Austin County Fair. I was only seventeen," she tells him. "Kent flew into the fairgrounds in a little plane, an Aeroscope I think it was. He was just starting out selling his rubber chicken plucking finger. He saw me in the Miss Fourth of July contest."

Wolfe gives her an appraising look.

"He kept flying back into Austin to see me," Dollye continues. "He was about twenty years older than me. Or eighteen, maybe. And then one time he took me and my sister and my mother on his plane to Chicago. And then when I turned eighteen, he married me."

Turbulence. Thump.

She clutches his arm.

Holds on a moment too long after the plane settles down.

Landing in Frankfurt, Wolfe and Dollye descend the stairs to the tarmac. He is the first member of his family to set foot on European soil since Doc escaped the Cossacks.

Emerging from customs, he is greeted by George Rosden, fifty-five, a lawyer and consultant with connections to European banks. Formal, Teutonic, Rosden clicks his heels when he lifts their luggage. He raises his eyebrows at Dollye, whose presence is completely unexpected.

He wheels a cart with their baggage to the curb, where a Volkswagen Beetle waits. Wolfe gestures at the frugal German in protest.

Wolfe: If I am going to meet your bankers, I have got to arrive like one.

He smokes a cigar, fuming, until Rosden returns in a Mercedes. He opens the back door for Wolfe and Dollye.

They drive to Zürich, arriving at the Grand Hotel Dolder, a five-star 1890s castle with magnificent views over Zürich, the lake, and the Alps. Wolfe signs for three rooms, one for himself, one for Dollye Tomlinson, and one for George Rosden. He asks to rent a safety deposit box.

The FBI reports that Wolfe "rented a safety deposit box at the hotel into which he placed fifteen to twenty packages which he had in a brief-case and which he told the hotel employee contained thousand-dollar bank notes of a total value of $4,000,000 to $5,000,000."[1]

Candles reflect off a window, lighting the reflections of Wolfe and Dollye, smoking, at a table in the Grand Hotel's dining room. Looking out the window, they see the snow-peaked mountains in the distance.

Wolfe: [reads from the menu] *Pate de foie gras, coq au vin, moules marinières. . . .*

Dollye: I don't know what any of those are.

Wolfe: Let's find out. We'll order all of them.

He beckons the waiter. Elegant in a cream dinner jacket, he impresses her with his savoir faire.

She is young and fresh, an intriguing combination of naive and knowing. She is his friend's wife. And she is twenty-five years younger than he is.

He escorts Dollye to her room, next to his. At the door, she thanks him for dinner, turns the key in the lock, slips inside.

After twenty-four hours of travel, the jet lag catches up with him. Wolfe soaks in a hot tub, cigar in one hand, glass of cognac in the other. He'll meet tomorrow with Rosden to set up meetings with the bankers.

A persistent rattling draws his attention. He lifts himself out of the tub, wraps himself in a luxuriant hotel robe. The sound comes from the door to the balcony. Through the window, he sees Dollye, in her night gown. He opens the door.

"Come out, y'all," she calls. "Look at the stars."

He joins her.

She shivers.

He puts his arm around her.

"C'mon, let's get a drink."

They go inside.

He pours them each a glass of cognac.

She slides up against him.

"I'm still cold. Hold me again."

He wraps his arms around her. She reaches up to wrap hers around his neck. Their sexual tension is loosed with a slow, passionate kiss.

His robe falls loose. She shrugs out of her night gown. They make love.

Later.

Dollye: This never happened, right?

Wolfe: No. We don't want any speeding tickets.

Zürich, October 8, 1958

Wolfe and Dollye ride in the back of the Mercedes driven by the German lawyer Rosden, en route to Paris to meet Kent, who is arriving from Chicago.

Wolfe is lost in thought. He puts his hand to his mouth. Her aroma has permeated his skin. He can taste her. She is sitting beside him, and he has so much he'd like to say but can't.

Rosden leaves them at the airport, off to Lichtenstein to set up a shell company.

Kent emerges from French customs and immigration. Dollye waves. Wolfe too.

When they meet, Kent sweeps her up in his arms, and she playfully pecks her husband's cheek. The men shake hands. Welcome to Europe.

The threesome takes the train to Monte Carlo. Their destination is the principality's famous casino.

Wolfe is in his element at the craps table, the feel for the dice a skill he acquired on the table in the back of Harry's Pool Room in Morden when he was a teenager. He's rolling in chips and raking in cash. Dollye watches him. He's a winner. She catches his eye.

"This one's for Dollye," he says, warming the dice in his hands. He rolls the dice, comes up a seven. He slides a pile of chips to Dollye. Excited, she hugs him. Her touch is electric. Kent raises his glass in a toast.

The whirlwind tour of Europe flies next to Rome, where they settle in at another luxury hotel. But not for long. They're off to see the Vatican, the Colosseum, the Spanish steps, all in a day.

Kent has a hankering to go to the world's fair in Brussels. He could develop the European market for rubber chicken plucker fingers. Dollye is disappointed. She wants to go to Venice.

"They say y'all haven't lived until y'all have been to Venice," she quotes an old saying. She pouts. Then she brightens.

"I have an idea. Wolfe can take me to Venice while y'all go to the world's fair."

Wolfe doesn't have to be convinced. But he makes a show of it. Protesting, he agrees to escort Dollye to Venice. Kent flies to Brussels.

From the files of the FBI:

Rabin and Mrs. Tomlinson left Rome by plane for Venice, but due
to weather conditions landed at Milan, Italy, where they stayed
overnight. Rabin and Mrs. Tomlinson took a train to Venice, Italy,
where they stayed for two or three days prior to their return to Milan
where they flew back to Zurich.[2]

Zürich, October 14, 1958

Wolfe returns to the Grand Hotel Dolder, where he retrieves his
envelopes from the safe, then to another hotel where he registers three
rooms, for Dollye, Rosden, and himself. He gives Dollye money to go
shopping.

The Mercedes pulls up under the hotel arches. Rosden gets out of
the driver's seat, comes around to open the back door for Wolfe. Clicks
his heels.

They drive east on the autobahn, high into the Alps until they
reach the German frontier. The guard at the checkpoint reviews their
documents.

As the Mercedes winds its way into Bavaria, Wolfe can't help from
reflecting on the war. *How can any Jew who visits Germany not feel*
conflicted? He prods Rosden.

Wolfe: So, you're the good German?

Rosden had been a civil court judge before the war. But his decisions
displeased the Nazis. He had been forced from office and prevented from
practicing law. But he refuses to be drawn out on the fate of the Jews.
Wolfe determines to use Rosden's introductions but not let the German
into his confidence.

The Mercedes drives through Munich with its gleaming new
International Style towers. The city has been rebuilt from the ravages of
Allied bombing, in part through the efforts of the man they are going to
meet, Dr. Theodore Siegel, a powerful banker and industrialist who made
a fortune in the postwar reconstruction.

In the investment banker's office, the fixer introduces Wolfe as an
industrialist from Chicago. Speaking in German, Rosden explains that

his client had made millions of dollars during World War II. And that he had transferred this money to Canada and bought first-class bearer bonds that were kept in different safe boxes in Canada. The problem was that this money hadn't been declared for taxes, and they need to find a way to fructify the bonds.

Wolfe tells the banker that he has decided the solution is to buy a bank. Or three banks, one in Switzerland, one in Germany, maybe a second in Germany or Lichtenstein. Would Dr. Siegel assist him in acquiring control of a bank?

The discussion continues over dinner of sauerbraten, schnitzel, and a chilled Riesling. Wolfe sends the waiter away with a lavish tip.

Wolfe raises his glass, looks the German banker in the eye. He asks Siegel if he would consider selling his bank. The financier is taken aback by the brash American.

Siegel: Definitely not. I've put my life into this bank. The bank is my life.

Wolfe: Think it over. This is a once-in-a-lifetime deal. My backers have *unlimited* sources of funds.

Siegel: Herr Rabin, I take you at face value. But my bank is not for sale.

While Wolfe is in Europe, a theft as stupendous as the Brockville Trust robbery goes off without a hitch at the National Guard Armory in Canton, Ohio. There is no apparent connection between the two headline stories.

Canton, Ohio, October 14, 1958

RAID OF OHIO NATIONAL GUARD ARMORY
300 Guns Are Stolen!!!
CANTON, Ohio (AP) More than 300 guns were stolen by burglars who broke into the National Guard Armory here Monday night. Police said the loot included 300 M-1 and carbine rifles, four .45 caliber submachine guns and eight .22-caliber bolt-action rifles.[3]

ARMORY RAID LAID TO CUBAN REBEL SYMPATHIZERS
KENT, O. (UPI)—Authorities believe the Canton raid was made by
Cuban rebel sympathizers because no one else could readily dispose of
such a quantity of arms. The FBI, meanwhile, investigated the Can-
ton burglary but has reported no new leads.

The robbers were believed to have hidden in the Canton armory
before it closed Monday. They forced open the supply room door and
wheeled gun racks to a side door where they apparently were loaded
into a truck.[4]

From the FBI files:

The informant, a New Jersey gun dealer, was contacted by the
operator of the Millville Ordnance Co., in Union, NJ, who said
he knew where a lot of M-1 rifles could be purchased. He told the
informant the rifles were hot and were part of the loot lifted from the
Canton Armory job in Ohio. He told the informant that the person
who had the guns from the Canton Armory wanted to get rid of them
and that in order to purchase the guns it would be necessary to meet
the seller in Washington, DC.[5]

Zürich, October 20–24, 1958

Wolfe and Dollye are curled up together in bed, sharing a postcoital
cigarette. The clock reads 2:00 a.m. The telephone rings.[6] Wolfe reaches
across Dollye, lifts the handset. She ducks under the twisted cord.

Hotel operator with an overseas call for Herr Rabin from Kent
Tomlinson in Chicago.

Wolfe sounds groggy. "Dollye? We said goodnight at her room after
dinner. She's asleep. Must have been that bottle of Burgundy we had."

Dollye, covers her lips, stifles a giggle.

Wolfe: Did you sell any pluckers in Brussels? I got a meeting in the
morning, it's after 2 a.m. here. Yeah, okay. G'night.

He reaches across Dollye to place the handset on the hook. She rolls on top, snuggling into his body.

At Leu & Company,[7] Switzerland's oldest bank, established in 1755, Wolfe is met by a committee of bank executives—Josef Frei, Dr. von Stockar, Herr Roesle, and Director Vogelsang. He pitches for a loan of 500,000 Swiss francs, outlining a proposal to invest in construction in Panama. If Castro and the communists take over Cuba, the casinos will close. The business will move to Panama. It's vintage Wolfe on a visionary high.

He assures them that the loan will be secured. Opening the satchel, he takes out a bundle of bonds.

The bankers inspect the certificates. Dr. von Stockar informs Rosden that the bank will first need to send the serial numbers to Canada for verification.

Rosden protests. His client has tax matters that need to remain confidential.

Rosden: Gentlemen, when I was the secretary of the Swiss Banking Association, I had to deal with many such titles that had disappeared in the course of the war. Many of these securities later reached Switzerland, shall we say, on "detours."

But the Swiss are determined to verify the bonds with the Canadian authorities. There is something about the Swiss bankers' attitude that disturbs Wolfe. It feels like the time he walked into a restricted club. He probes.

Wolfe: You weren't so precise about provenance during the war, were you?

Dr. von Stockar: What do you mean, Herr Rabin?

Wolfe: You know what I mean. The *gelt*. All the money in your vaults that belongs to the Jews who were murdered.

The Swiss are stunned.

Wolfe stuffs the bonds back into his satchel and storms out. Rosden backpedals.

The Mercedes arrives at the Basel headquarters of the Credit Suisse, a bank so powerful that international financial stability depends on it.[8]

Wolfe and the fixer Rosden play their scene with the bankers, an improvisational work in progress.

Wolfe: May we rely on your discretion?

Rosden: Mr. Rabin has accumulated a great amount of money that is invested at the present time in partly registered Canadian dollar bonds.

Wolfe: We're going to use the funds to buy surplus ships from the U.S. Navy. I'm starting a line to run freight in the Caribbean.

Wolfe makes the proposal to pledge bonds for working capital for the project. The Credit Suisse bankers are receptive. Wolfe negotiates a deal for the bonds, receiving US $470,000 cash and 170,000 Swiss francs.

He celebrates with Rosden and a glass of schnapps. In his suite, Wolfe places calls to numbers in Pittsburgh and Miami. He leaves messages. The financing is in place.

Walking through the hotel lobby, Wolfe carries Dollye's valise.

Dollye: What does this mean, Wolfe? Are we just shipmates on a cruise?

Wolfe: No, no, I love you. But you know I have responsibilities.

Dollye: And I have my two boys.

Wolfe: Okay, you make the rules.

Dollye looks him in the eyes.

Then it's a level playing field.

Through the main doors to the driveway, where Wolfe flags a taxi, helps her into the car.

Wolfe: Have a safe flight. Say hello to Kent.

He mouths the words, "I love you."

At the hotel gift shop, Wolfe buys postcards, plasters them with stamps, addresses them to his nephew in Montreal. No message. Just the stamps. For the kid's collection.

Zürich is one of the most important global trading centers for precious metals. Wolfe taxis to the Cartier boutique on the Bahnhofstrasse. He selects a gold tank watch for himself and an exquisite pair of diamond earrings. Small items of high value aren't likely to arouse the customs inspectors. He peels more thousand-dollar bills from his money clip for the purchases.

Swissair first class back across the Atlantic.

Not a bad commute. What a trip! Made the bonds deal and fell in lust with the most beautiful young woman. His new muse. He could get used to this.

On his return to New York, Wolfe goes to a currency broker in Manhattan. He sells some of the Swiss francs he received in Zürich in exchange for the bonds, walking away with $29,000 cash. Easy.

There are 8 million stories in the Naked City. This has been one of them. —Naked City, television series, 1959

Coast of Cuba, October 1958

Night. The moon obscured by clouds. A small boat quietly glides into the dock at the Dupont estate on the Cuban coast. Two men jump onto the dock, Joe Merola and a Cuban. Merola climbs up to the cockpit of a twin-engine Beechcraft moored at the dock. It's not locked. They never are.

Small planes have key ignitions just like cars. They can be even easier to hotwire. At a signal, the man on the dock slips the plane from its moorings. The pilot closes the circuit, the propellers turn, and the Beech taxis out on the pontoons.

Within weeks, five private airplanes are stolen along the coast.

From the files of the FBI:

With Joseph Merola as a passenger, pilot Stuart Sutor left the Miami International Airport in the twin-engine Beechcraft on October 24, 1958, for the Allegheny Airport. Stuart Sutor considers himself a "soldier of fortune" and examination of his personal log book verifies the fact that he has logged hundreds of hours in the air in North and South America, as well as in the Far East.[9]

After Sutor and Merola landed at Allegheny Airport, they took a cab to Merola's sister's house in the Regent Square section of Pittsburgh and borrowed her car. They drove to the Tour-Tel Motel on U.S. Route 92 where they registered for the night. Merola and Sutor then traveled to New Kensington, where Merola attempted to locate Sam Mannarino.[10]

Vatican City, October 28, 1958

White smoke puffs from the chimney at the Vatican, signifying the selection of a new leader of the Roman Catholic Church. Cardinal Angelo Giuseppe Roncalli is elected, taking the name Pope John XXIII. Father Nicola Fusco of Mount St. Peter's in New Kensington attends the conclave, his travel arrangements courtesy the Mannarino brothers.

Chapter Seven

Air Chase

Guns to Cuba

New Kensington, Pennsylvania, November 4, 1958

A FADED SIGN CLINGING TO A CHAIN-LINK FENCE IDENTIFIES THE KEN Iron and Steel Company. The scrap-metal yard is a four-acre war zone of the detritus of industrial America.

Sam Mannarino peers at the yard through the blinds. His office is cluttered with salvaged appliances, files spilling from cabinets. The telephone rings, he picks up, listens, grunts. Points across the room at a punk in a leather coat with a greased-back pompadour. His son-in-law, Victor Carlucci, twenty-two.

Mannarino waves him out of the office. "Don't fuck up."

Victor runs through the scrapyard, beckoning a driver with Elvis-style ducktail leaning against the hood of a white truck, smoking. Victor slaps him on the shoulder. "Speedo, get moving." Speedo climbs into the cab of the truck, slams the door lettered S & S Distributing Company. The truck lurches out the gates followed by a Ford with Victor behind the wheel.

Air Traffic Control, Buffalo, New York

In the command center of the U.S. Border Patrol, agents' eyes are trained on the radar screens tracking a plane flying across western Pennsylvania. Losing altitude, the object of their interest appears to be landing.

An aqua and white Beechcraft C-18 touches down at the Allegheny Valley Airport near the hamlet of Tarentum, Pennsylvania. The plane wheels around, comes to a halt by the hangar. The pilot Stuart Sutor, thirty-three, in leather bomber jacket, climbs down from the plane.

The white truck and the Ford arrive at the small airfield, screeching up to the plane. The car doors open, Victor and Sutor step out. Walking from the plane, Sutor approaches. Victor recognizes him. It's Sutor's second run.

Speedo opens the truck gate, and the men begin unloading large, heavy burlap bags. They heft them up onto the plane, where the seats have been removed behind the cockpit to make more cargo space. Grunting and sweating, it takes an hour to load the cargo onto the plane.

From the tall grasses at the edge of the airfield, a man with binoculars watches the burlap bags being loaded. He turns to the trooper standing next to him. The trooper crouches through the grass, heads toward a patrol car pulled low into the culvert.

Sutor climbs into the cockpit, pulls up the steps, closes the door. He fires up the engines, flashes a thumbs-up. The Beechcraft taxis down the airstrip. A state patrol car races into the airfield as the white truck with Speedo at the wheel and the Ford with Victor escape the opposite direction. Running onto the field, the agent who had been watching through the binoculars frantically waves his arms. More patrol cars arrive.

Airborne, Sutor looks down at the scene below. Close one. He pushes the plane harder. An engine sputters. Checks the gauges. Low fuel.

He spots a place to put down, another small airstrip. He lands, rolling the plane up to the fuel pumps. A grizzled attendant in coveralls shuffles over from the Quonset hut. Notes the name on the fuselage. Transit Flasher Company.

Attendant: Not from around here?

Sutor shakes his head. The guy is full of questions. Where you coming from? Where you headed? Sutor desperately needs to take a leak. Fill 'er up, he tells the attendant. Asks for the john, goes to relieve himself.

The fuel comes to $37.80. Sutor gives the attendant a $100 bill. He goes to the office. Takes a long time. Returns, apologetic, he can't make change for a hundred. Okay, keep it for next time. Ignoring the attendant's protests, the pilot climbs back into the cockpit, revs up.

The blip on the radar screens that is the Beechcraft takes off, heading south.

In the cockpit, Sutor sees a Piper Commanche approaching from starboard. Sutor accelerates, but the Beechcraft lumbers along, burdened by the weight of its cargo. The Piper flies close enough for Sutor to see the U.S. Border Patrol shields on the plane. Closer. Signaling him to put down.

Police vehicles line the airstrip at Morgantown, West Virginia. FBI agents and sheriff's deputies crouch behind their cars, guns drawn. Sutor lands the Beechcraft on the strip in front of them. The Border Patrol plane lands right behind.

SEIZED ARMS, SAID STOLEN FROM ARMORY

MORGANTOWN, W. VA.—Arms found on board the Beechcraft C-18, captured shortly after noon yesterday at the Morgantown Municipal Airport, have been definitely identified as part of those stolen from a Canton, Ohio, National Guard Armory.

The plane was captured yesterday by local State and County Police as it was being refueled here for a flight on to Florida and a rendezvous with Fidel Castro's Cuban rebels. The pilot, Stuart Sutor, 34, seemed a bit disgusted at the time of his arrest. "I've flown all over the world," he said, "and here I am caught by a bunch of hillbillies."[1]

Chicago, November 5, 1958

A room service waiter delivers coffee and the morning newspaper to Wolfe and Trudy in their suite. The peripatetic couple move from one apartment-hotel to another every few weeks. Often just ahead of the overdue rent.

Wolfe grips the newspaper, intent on the photograph of the pilot and the Beechcraft on the front page.

SEIZED ARMS LINKED TO ALLEGED RACKETEER

PITTSBURGH (UPI) Federal authorities pressed their investigation into a gun-smuggling operation which was broken up when the Border Patrol intercepted a shipment of rifles stolen from a Canton, Ohio, National Guard Armory and apparently being flown to rebel forces in Cuba.

At Pittsburgh, three men, including the son-in-law of reputed racket figure Sam Mannarino, were freed on their own recognizance after questioning by the Federal Bureau of Investigation.

Federal authorities disclosed still another link with the Mannarinos. They said a federal agent and a state policeman had watched the plane being loaded at the Allegheny Valley Airport, near Tarentum, from a truck registered in the name of the S & S Distributing Co., a firm owned by Sam Mannarino's brother Gabriel.[2]

Guns from the army. An air force to ferry them. Bad luck about the truck. As Wolfe considers the implications, the telephone rings. The operator has a collect call from Herr Rosden in Lichtenstein. "Will Mr. Rabin accept the charges?" Rosden is in a panic. Credit Suisse is questioning the validity of the bonds.

The Swiss bank wants more than the $78,000 it loaned to Wolfe. The bank demands the face value of the bonds, in full. Wolfe stalls.

Wolfe tells Rosden to write to them that all will be whole once the Cuban Revolution is over. "There will be more money than you can count. Tell them we'll pay them in pesos."

He tells Rosden to remind the bank of its reputation for discretion. Neither Wolfe nor Credit Suisse would like this transaction to be subject to public scrutiny. He directs Rosden to ask the bank if it will be acceptable for him to replace the unverifiable bonds with legitimate ones. He will need time to make arrangements.

Washington, D.C., November 10, 1958

The telephone rings at the office of the FBI in the Department of Justice. Agent George Benjamin takes the call from the vice president of a large D.C. bank who is calling to advise that a neighbor of his, George Rosden, approached him stating he represented a client who desired to pledge some bonds. He asked the banker if a deposit certificate could be given for the bonds that could thereafter be pledged for a loan.

He told Rosden the arrangement couldn't be made. It's been on his mind, so he is calling the bureau.

Benjamin turns to his partner, senior agent Jim Ryan. Could this be connected to the stolen Canadian bonds? They call Rosden, who states that "he would not have made this approach to Mr. Bergman had he known the bonds were stolen because he would not want to take advantage of his friend and the Riggs Bank."[3]

Montreal, November 25, 1958

Pep Cotroni drives Wolfe to the Bonfire Restaurant, a drive-in pizza hangout. "I got a piece of this place," he confides. Wolfe opens the car door, but Cotroni waves him back. They will eat in the car, more confidential. Cotroni flashes the headlights. A waitress appears, hooks a tray onto the open window.

Wolfe puts his cards on the table. He needs to make good to the Swiss bank for the bonds.

Cotroni reminds Wolfe of his cash-only policy. For Mannarino's friend, he will make an exception. He will give Wolfe more bonds to trade. Sell them, and he can pay his way out. It will require a few days to organize the bonds. They will come from the same source, all legitimate bearer bonds. It's a fool's bargain, but it's all he's got. Wolfe should wait for a call at his hotel in New York.

Wolfe invites his sister Ruby for drinks at the Mount Royal. She is back on her feet, writing copy for a Montreal advertising agency. He spins tales of his trip to Europe, of castles and palaces and sojourns in grand hotels. He is in fine form, until Ruby tells him to cut the shit and tell her what he's up to.

He has got a new career, he explains. He has found his calling as an international bonds trader.

Ruby: What do you know about trading bonds?

Wolfe: There's a fortune to be made, I know that.

Ruby: Don't you need a broker's license?

Wolfe: My banker suggested that!

New York City, December 4, 1958

Empty bottles from the minibar litter the dresser in Wolfe's room at the Edison. Wolfe lights a cigarette, stares at the telephone. He places a call to Cotroni's number in Montreal, but there is no answer. The television draws his attention.

Senator John McClellan (on television):

The coin-operated machine industry has been forced to deal with racketeers and to pay tribute to them for the right to stay in business. The stakes are very high. The revenue from these machines reaches over 2 billion dollars a year.[4]

Live from a committee room in the Old Senate Office Building in Washington, all three networks broadcast hearings of the Senate committee exposing racketeering and organized crime.

Senator John McClellan (on television):

Among the witnesses that we shall have today will be racket figures from various parts of the country who have shown an interest in the coin-operated machine industry. That these underworld figures do come from widely scattered areas is no accident, because there is virtually no area in the United States in which they have not at least made an effort to gain a foothold in this industry.[5]

Wolfe asks the operator for a Pittsburgh number, gets Mannarino on the phone, tells him to turn on the television. The shit has hit the fan.

Chicago, December 21, 1958

At Western Union, Wolfe counts $10,000 from the cash he pocketed for selling the bonds at the currency broker in New York. He wires the funds to the Swiss financial giant in Basel. Should keep them off his back.

Behind his back, the wires are humming. The transfer arouses suspicions at the international clearinghouse in Montreal. Credit Suisse sends a list of serial numbers of Canadian bonds for verification. Teletypes hammer out the response: the serial numbers match those on a list of bonds stolen from the Brockville Trust. The Canadians demand to know who sold the bonds to Credit Suisse, but the Swiss are not about to reveal that information. Their priority is the money.

The RCMP issues a bulletin alerting Interpol and the FBI to the Swiss lead. Marked high priority, it comes across the wire in the Chicago bureau of the FBI and is assigned to agent Robert Malone, forty-three, to investigate. Who is laundering the bonds? How did they get them? The Swiss know, but they aren't telling.

Chicago, December 26, 1958

Wolfe meets with Frank Pepe at the Central National Bank to request an extension on his loan against the bonds. He gets a thirty-day reprieve. The loan officer pours Wolfe a brandy, compliments of the season.

Wolfe makes his way to his car through a blizzard.

Through the cold winter sky, Wolfe and Kent Tomlinson fly in the Cessna to Montreal, where they overnight, and then are joined by Pep Cotroni and his flunky René Savard. Crammed in the little plane, they clear customs at Buffalo and fly on to Flushing Field in Queens. The cadre taxi across New York to Idlewyld, where they board a flight to Florida.

Miami, December 28, 1958

The humidity engulfs Wolfe on his arrival at Dade County Airport. The four men wait at the curb, a car pulls up, the driver beckons, they exit the airport parkway.

Sam Mannarino and Norman Rothman are waiting for them in the bar at the Sea Gull, a boomerang-styled motel on the beach.

Television news behind the bar. Rebels coming down from the hills. Cuban army deserting, defecting.

A stentorian voice narrates over the black-and-white film:

The eyes of Cuba have been focused on the Sierra Maestra for the past 14 months, the zone in which the band of Fidel Castro is playing hide-and-seek. It is known that the rebel who crosses the wilds of the Sierra Maestra in search of an avenue of escape from his pursuers maintains strong bonds with the Communist Party which operates clandestinely on the island.[6]

Three columns of armed guerillas have reached the central provinces and are within striking distance of Havana. The bearded rebel leader vows to end corruption and racketeering and take control of Cuba by Cubans. Batista's army is running or defecting to the revolution.

The casinos in Havana are at risk. The men gathered at the Sea Gull need to protect their interests.

Miami, December 30, 1958

Four men in fashionable suits wearing dark glasses cross the tarmac at Miami airport and mount the stairs to a Pan Am propjet. From the tower, a long lens brings each into focus, and a shutter clicks. Sam Mannarino. "Pep" Cotroni. "Roughhouse" Rothman. And the fourth man, who will later be identified as William "Wolfe" Rabin.

The men settle comfortably in first class for the forty-five-minute flight to Havana. A curvaceous stewardess offers drinks from a tray.

Mannarino nudges Wolfe beside him.

> Mannarino: Did you hear the one about the stewardess who asked a flasher to show his boarding pass? When he opened his trench coat, she said, "Sir, I need to see your ticket, not your stub!"

Guffaws. The stewardess blushes. She "accidentally" spills a drink on Mannarino's shirt. Wolfe hides a chuckle.

REVOLUTION

Havana, December 31, 1958

In just two years, Havana has seen an explosion in the construction of hotel-casinos along the Malecon, all of them controlled by organized crime syndicates.[7] Meyer Lansky opens the fabulous Riviera. His brother Jake runs the Hotel Nacional. Movie star George Raft has a piece of the Capri. The Havana Hilton is run by a syndicate who take over the assets of the assassinated gangster Albert Anastasia. The Deauville is a boutique jewel built by Santo Trafficante, who controls the Tropicana, the grande dame of the casinos.

A limo with Wolfe and his business associates cruises through the streets of Havana. Wolfe points his 16mm camera through the window, rushing through the eerily quiet streets of the capital, only a few passing police cruisers and olive drab Cuban army vehicles.

He thinks back to the first time he flew here with Trudy, when he was the jukebox maestro. Havana was a smaller, more romantic place then. This will be their first New Year's Eve apart since they've been married. A brief memory. But it's Dollye he can't get out of his mind. *A gnawing regret grinds in the pit of his stomach. How did it get to this?* The limo arrives at the Tropicana. *Snap out of it.*

Bargain airfares, comped rooms, and tickets to floor shows lure thousands of Americans and Europeans to welcome the New Year in Havana despite the smoke of revolution in the air. Inside the casinos, they party in a parallel universe of gambling, drinking, and whoring, a contrast to the Cuba of poverty and illiteracy outside the gates.

Just past midnight, the bombs begin exploding. At first, the crowd in the casino takes the sound to be more New Year's cannons and continues gambling. Then there is an ear-shattering thud, and the lights go out. Rothman grabs Wolfe, they run to the counting room.

Rothman orders the staff to collect all the money in the casino, all the cash, empty the safety deposit boxes, just the U.S. cash. He snatches a telephone, but the line is dead. They grab sacks of money and race down concrete stairs to the garage.

People are taking to the streets. Bombs explode in the distance. Sporadic gunfire erupts, closer. The mood of celebration turns to violence. People start hacking at the parking meters, knowing that every centavo goes into the corrupt President Batista's pocket.

A sedan makes its way through the mayhem and confusion. Inside the car, Wolfe drives, keeps his head down. Rothman draws his gun.

The rampaging mob surges into the casinos, symbols of foreign exploitation of Cuba. Machine gun fire shatters the chandelier in the Riviera, panic among the revelers. Slot machines are torn out and battered, even the jukeboxes are destroyed. Roulette wheels and craps tables are dragged from the casinos and set on fire. A truckload of pigs is set loose in the lobby of the Riviera, squealing, tracking mud, and defecating across the floors.[8]

The crowd pelts the Americans' car with rocks, the windows shatter but don't break. Wolfe and Rothman emerge unscathed. Rothman smashes out the windshield with the butt of his gun so Wolfe can see the road ahead. Avoiding roadblocks and demonstrators carrying the red and black flag of the revolution, the car winds its way up to Miramar. Arriving at the gates of a villa, armed men shine flashlights in their eyes. Rothman speaks in Spanish, and they are waved in.

Every mobster in Havana that night has made his way to the mansion of "Hoboken Joe" Stassi, general fixer and arbiter among the crime syndicates that control Havana's casinos and its underworld.

According to a witness, "There were guns all over the room, on tabletops, on the floor, in shoulder holsters, and tucked into waistbands. There were mounds of cash in the living room of Stassi's estate. Money was being divided into equal denominations and distributed among the mobsters."[9]

New York City, January 2, 1959

Snow falls outside LaGuardia Airport where Wolfe, still in his tropical-weight suit, stands in line for customs clearance. He takes a cigarette case from his breast pocket, lights a Pall Mall. His turn. The usual routine. Purpose of your trip? He pats the satchel. Business.

The customs agent orders Wolfe to open his briefcase. He raises his eyebrows, waits a beat before complying. The agent looks inside, finds a *Herald-Tribune* headlining the Cuban revolution, two freshly laundered shirts, a shaving kit, a businessman's diary, a copy of *Exodus*, the bestseller by Leon Uris, and a box of Monte Cristos.

The customs officer checks Wolfe's declaration. The cigars are on it. He looks up, smiles at Wolfe, stuffs everything back in the satchel. Welcome to New York. Better get a warm coat.

A warm surprise greets him when he arrives in Manhattan.

From the files of the FBI: "Mr. and Mrs. Rabin registered at Warwick Hotel, New York City, and stayed until January 4, 1959 [the Mrs. Rabin registered believed to be Dollye Tomlinson]."[10]

Chicago, January 1959

By the time Wolfe returns to Chicago, Trudy is growing royally pissed at him, and she has been drinking.

"There's someone else, isn't there!" she accuses. "I can smell her perfume on your clothes!"

Pittsburgh, January 22, 1959

A highly placed informant—"a former top hoodlum of the Pittsburgh office and one-time officer in the Sans Souci Night Club, Havana"—calls the FBI to fink on Sam Mannarino. Mannarino engineered the theft of firearms from the National Guard Armory in Canton, the informer reports, but is being shunned by the "racket element" for his foolishness in becoming involved in the undertaking. He speculates that Mannarino fingered the burglary of the armory without the knowledge or consent of his brother Gabe.[11]

Chicago, January 24, 1959

At the Western Union wicket, Wolfe reaches into his pocket for his money clip, counts another ten $1,000 bills, slides the forms and the cash across to the clerk. He issues instructions to wire the funds to an account at Credit Suisse in Basel. Buying time.

He has drinks with his brother Leon, who is in business for himself manufacturing electric eyes for garage door openers. He gives Leon a key to the safety deposit box—in case something should happen to him. There is something Wolfe doesn't want to reveal. Leon yearns to ask, but his concerns remain unspoken.

FBI agent Robert Malone receives a response to his alert for cash transfers. A Western Union clerk calls to report sending a wire for $10,000 to Credit Suisse. Malone calls every bank in Chicago, requests records of all transfers to Switzerland.

CHAPTER EIGHT

Front Page

SENATE HEARINGS
Chicago, February 10, 1959

Trudy turns on the television in the hotel suite, changes channels looking for *The Edge of Night*, her favorite soap opera. But it's been preempted. All three networks are broadcasting the organized crime hearings from the Senate in Washington.

At the bar, she pours a glass of scotch. Lights cigarette. Bored, she starts watching the hearings, growing intrigued by the attractive man asking the questions. Sounds just like Senator Kennedy. The speaker turns out to be the senator's younger brother Robert Kennedy, thirty-two, the committee's counsel, about to make a name for himself as chief inquisitor.

Described by one biographer as tough, competitive, suspicious, and tightly wound,[1] the charismatic Kennedy is lightning in a cathode-ray tube. Trudy is riveted. This is better than the soap opera.

Kennedy has assembled the largest investigating team ever to work on Capitol Hill. He subpoenas powerful racketeers to testify. Facing the committee on the dais, keeping his cool under the television lights, the witness in tailored gray sharkskin suit is the dapper don Michael Genovese, consigliere to the Pittsburgh branch of La Cosa Nostra. From the transcript of the Senate's *Investigation of Improper Activities in the Labor or Management Field*[2]:

Kennedy: You were a close associate of Sam Mannarino; is that right?

The mobster stares at his manicured nails, as though considering.

Genovese: I respectfully decline.

The introduction of Mannarino's name draws Trudy's undivided attention. Why is Wolfe's partner from the jukebox company involved in the hearings?

On television, Kennedy continues his interrogation of the mobster.

Kennedy: The guns that were being flown to Cuba recently, guns that had been stolen from an armory in Ohio, when the plane was apprehended, those guns were being sent by Mr. Mannarino, were they not?

Genovese: I respectfully decline to answer.

Kennedy: They were being sent in connection with the revolution in Cuba.

Genovese: I respectfully decline to answer.

Kennedy: Do you know anything about that?

Genovese confers with his counsel, Pittsburgh lawyer Vincent Casey, sixty, partner of the recently deceased Charlie Margiotti.

Genovese: I respectfully decline to answer.

Kennedy: Is it not correct that you own a farm near the airport where the guns were placed on the plane?

Genovese: I respectfully decline to answer.

Kennedy: Could you tell us why you went into the coin-operating machine business?

Genovese: I respectfully decline to answer.

Kennedy: Could you tell us if the coin-operating machine business was discussed at the meeting at Apalachin?

Genovese: I respectfully decline to answer.

Loud knocking at the door interrupts. Trudy peers through the peephole. Agent Malone flashes a badge. FBI. Her heart pounds.

TANGLED WEB
Washington, D.C., February 12, 1959
The FBI mobilizes its investigation into the missing Canadian bonds. The story continues to draw headlines as details leak. Agents George Benjamin and Jim Ryan pay an unannounced visit to George Rosden at his office on F Street. From their report of his interview:

> *Rosden stated that he had gathered from his conversations with Rabin that he had received these bonds from a representative of the Cuban rebels in payment for services in connection with securing arms for the Cubans.*
>
> *Rosden was particularly pressed for money at the time, and thus Rabin seemed like a "messenger from heaven."*[3]

New York, February 13, 1959
Smoking a cigarette, Wolfe waits in the Swissair lounge at Idlewild for the flight to Zürich. At a pay phone, he asks the operator for a Chicago number, station to station. Drops quarters into the slot.

Trudy answers. She's frantic.

Trudy: Where are you? The FBI came here looking for you. Are you in trouble?

Wolfe: Must be a misunderstanding.

Trudy: Has this got to do with those hearings on television?

Wolfe: I sure hope not.

He reassures her that there must be a mistake and gets off the phone. Leaves the gate. The flight agent calls after him, but he doesn't turn back.

Washington, DC, February 13, 1959

The Eastern Airlines shuttle descends past the Washington Monument. At National Airport, Wolfe hails a taxi, asks the driver to show him the sights. The Lincoln Memorial. The Jefferson Monument. The White House. He is overcome by unexpected feelings of patriotism. He had taken out American citizenship in 1937, a vow he took to heart.

He riffles through his diary, gives the driver an address on F Street. Scanning the building directory, he finds the law office of George Eric Rosden, the German fixer. Asks the elevator operator to take him to the fifth floor.

Rosden is disconcerted at Wolfe's unscheduled arrival. And upset by the FBI sniffing around.

He demands to know where Wolfe got the bonds. Wolfe tells him they were payment for his consulting services, from a man named Garcia. Rosden asks Wolfe if he has been buying guns to send to the rebels in Cuba.

Wolfe: I haven't bought any guns. I went to Europe to arrange for shipping the guns.
Rosden: Credit Suisse is pushing hard to get the bonds redeemed.

But Wolfe is concerned about a more imminent threat. Since the FBI only wants to talk to him, he will take them by surprise. And he will bring his lawyer with him. He insists Rosden come with him, drags him protesting from the office.

Department of Justice, Same Day

Wolfe steps out of a taxi at FBI headquarters, while Rosden meticulously counts the change. Wolfe takes a deep breath, urges the reluctant Rosden along. They enter through a revolving door.

Special agents George Benjamin and James Ryan, the same pair who had visited Rosden's office, usher them into a room with a mirror on one wall. The FBI agents question Wolfe. One reads aloud from his notepad.

Agent: You accepted the bonds as collateral for your consulting work. Is that your statement?

Before Wolfe can respond, a secretary enters, passes a folded note to the lead agent. He motions Rosden to leave the room with him.[4]

In the corridor, the agent asks Rosden if he is Rabin's lawyer.

Rosden: I represent Mr. Rabin on certain business matters. But I am not a criminal lawyer.

Agent: Then he'd better get one.

They return to the interrogation room. The agent informs Wolfe that the district attorney in Chicago has directed them to arrest Wolfe.

He decides it would be pointless to antagonize the agents, better to spin out the narrative from his perspective. From the files of the FBI:

> *He related considerable background information and details concerning his receiving $2,500,000 in Canadian Government bonds from one Alfredo Garcia, a representative of Cuban rebels, which bonds were to be taken to Europe by Rabin. In Europe Rabin would deliver these bonds in three separate packages to secret agents who would identify themselves by the number 26. One package was to be delivered in Zurich, Switzerland, one in Rome, Italy, and one in Venice, Italy. For this Rabin received $5,000 in cash and $266,000 in Canadian Government bonds.*
>
> *Rabin stated that after leaving the train in Milan Italy, he was met by an individual, who identified himself as "26." He accompanied this person to the washroom and delivered package number three to him.[5]*

Wolfe is charged with receiving stolen bonds. He is booked, fingerprinted, and photographed. FBI agents escort him to a courtroom, where the charge is read aloud by the commissioner. He pleads not guilty. The judge sets bail at $5,000.

Wolfe reaches into his pocket for his money clip and counts out five $1,000 bills. He steps forward and hands the money to the judge.

Wolfe: Will that do, your Honor?

The FBI agent is outraged.

Benjamin: What are you doing with that kind of money?

Judge: Yes, Mr. Rabin, please tell the court why you are carrying such a large sum.

Wolfe: I'd feel naked traveling with anything less, your Honor.

The judge does a double take before responding. As Wolfe turned himself in and has been very cooperative, bail is granted. Agents Benjamin and Ryan protest but the judge waves them off. Wolfe is free to go.[6]

A wire service photographer captures Wolfe as he exits the courtroom.

From the pay phone in the lobby, he places a collect call to Norman Rothman at the Warwick Hotel in New York.

"Cover your tracks, Normie," he advises. "The FBI are everywhere."[7]

Chicago, February 14, 1959

Trudy brandishes the newspaper with Wolfe's picture on the front page in one hand, holds the telephone in the other.

Trudy: This is one hell of a Valentine's Day present! Did you steal the bonds?

Wolfe: No, I didn't steal the bonds. And when I found out they were stolen, I started to pay them back with my own money.[8]

Trudy: Then how did you get the bonds?

Wolfe: They were payment for a consulting deal.

Trudy: I don't know if I should believe you.

Wolfe: I got them from a guy named Garcia.

Trudy: Your picture is on the front page. What is your family going to say?!

HOW MYSTERY MAN GOOFED PERFECT CRIME
A blunder by William W. Rabin, 52, a mysterious globe-trotting financier, after a "perfect crime," led to his indictment with four

gangsters on charges of plotting to sell stolen Canadian bonds worth
14 million dollars, federal authorities disclosed Friday.

Rabin, a former Chicago jukebox distributor, makes frequent
plane trips to France and Switzerland where, according to the indict-
ments, he pledged stolen bonds valued at $140,000 to buy a bank to
convert the bulk of the Brockville loot.[9]

The morning paper lies open on the kitchen table in a Chicago mansion. Stella Lamperti, fifty-one, the mother of Wolfe's love child, now a wife and mother and an accomplished artist, sits down for a morning coffee. She lights a cigarette. Drawn to Wolfe's photo on the front page, she slides the newspaper over, gasps. She leans over to read, rapt in the exploits of her old boyfriend.

Her husband Michael enters on his way to the back door, leans over Stella to see what has got her transfixed.

"Someone I used to know," she offers.

Michael raises his eyebrow, gives her a peck on the cheek. He's on his way to a meeting with some Democratic Party officials. They want him to run for the state senate.

Stella hears the car back out of the garage. She takes a scissors from the kitchen counter, carefully clips the story about Wolfe.

Chicago, February 16, 1959

FBI agent Robert Malone has been tracking Wolfe's wire transactions. He calls in his colleague Ed Kinzer, thirty-five, a navy veteran with a law degree. Kinzer is a keener; once he gets his teeth into a case, he won't let go. Examining Wolfe's itinerary obtained from the travel agent, they decide to interview Wolfe's traveling companions, Kent and Dollye Tomlinson—separately.

Kent shows up at the FBI offices, looks and sounds like Jimmy Stewart. Aw, shucks. He tells them about the trip to Europe, meeting his wife and Wolfe in Paris. Traveling to Monte Carlo and Rome. All the sights, the Eiffel Tower, the Vatican, the Colosseum. They didn't do any business.

The detectives want to know about the payments Wolfe had made to Kent Industries and the Kent Tomlinson Company.

"Rabin was repaying loans I had given him a few years back," Kent explains.[10]

The next day, Dollye responds to the FBI summons. Mindful of her southern manners, the agents are duly respectful. But they insist on probing her relationship with Wolfe. Had he been given instructions to go to Venice?

"Where did y'all get that from? It was my idea to go to Venice," she says. Malone takes notes.

Kinzer asks if Wolfe had met an agent with the code name 26.

"He didn't meet with anyone," Dollye responds. "He was with me all the time."

Kinzer: But the hotel records show that you weren't in the same hotel room as Rabin in Venice.

Dollye: Honey, like I told y'all, he was never out of my sight.

Malone tells Dollye they may need to call her to testify before a grand jury.

Dollye: Now why would I do that? I am not going to testify in front of a grand jury or any other jury. I don't need that kind of publicity.

Ladies and gentlemen, the story you are about to see is true. Only the names have been changed to protect the innocent. —Dragnet, *television series, 1959*

Chicago, February 19, 1959

FBI agents Malone and Kinzer and an agent from the Internal Revenue Service barge into the offices of the Rek Chemical Company, a Mannarino front in a warehouse on South Michigan Avenue. The G-men flash their badges. Malone demands to know where William Rabin works. A distraught middle-aged woman points to a darkened corner office, blinds drawn.

The detectives ransack the office, turning everything inside out and upside down. A man demands to see a search warrant.

Malone: Who are you kidding? You watch too much television.

The lower left drawer of Wolfe's desk yields a large manila envelope containing Government of Canada bonds. Nine bonds, face value $1,000 each. Malone handles them with care, the bonds will need to be dusted for prints.

At the bureau, Malone compares the serial numbers on the nine bonds found in Wolfe's desk with a list of the bonds taken in the Brockville blast. The numbers match.

Pittsburgh, February 1959

Wolfe arrives in Pittsburgh. On his way out to New Kensington to meet with Sam Mannarino, he stops at the Carlton House Hotel. Looking around the lobby, a tall, thin man signals Wolfe to join him.

Harry Savage is a lawyer who wears two hats. He is an assistant district attorney for Allegheny County while maintaining a lucrative private practice. Wolfe and Savage are acquainted from the lawyer's time as an associate with the firm of Margiotti & Casey when Charlie Margiotti was chairman of the board of National Filben, the jukebox company that had flamed out over patent rights.

"Everything I tell you is off the record, right?" Wolfe asks.

Savage confirms. The case is all over the headlines, he is eager to hear the inside story.

Wolfe tells the lawyer that he got the bonds from the Cuban agent Alfredo Garcia. He lets slip that the weapons stolen from the National Guard Armory were intended for the Cuban president, Fulgencio Batista, and not for Castro and the rebels.

The lawyer is all ears. "Go on, tell me more."

Drawing him closer, Wolfe confides that Sam Mannarino could cripple his son-in-law, Victor Carlucci, for bungling the loading operation. That's what got the pilot busted.

Wolfe is going to meet with Sam. He tells Savage that he might consult him professionally in the future about organizing his defense.[11]

Miami, February 28, 1959

Agent John Lenihan of the FBI's Miami office drives over to Surfside to pay a visit to Norman Rothman. The Capper is always cooperative with the law. He tells Lenihan that "Rabin reached him by telephone in Havana, in either December 1958 or early January 1959, when Rabin asked him to locate a Cuban named Alfredo Garcia who had fouled up Rabin in the business deal." Rothman explains, as though the FBI man had never read his file, that in the last few years of the Batista regime, he was in the gambling business in Cuba, which was why Rabin had wanted him to locate Garcia.

The big man shrugs. So far, he has been unsuccessful in locating Garcia. He'll be sure to call if the mysterious Cuban shows up.[12]

The FBI and the CIA expend considerable time and resources attempting to track down the elusive Alfredo Garcia, who seems to have vanished into thin air.

New York City, February 28, 1959

Smoking, drinking, Wolfe waits in his room at the Warwick in New York. Waiting for the call. He turns on the television, adjusts the rabbit ears.

Mike Wallace (on television):

> One of the nation's most powerful gang leaders, Abner "Longy" Zwillman, ended his life by hanging today. His body was found in the basement of his home in West Orange, New Jersey.
>
> Zwillman was known as the Al Capone of New Jersey. He was one of the top figures in the jukebox and coin machine rackets and was under subpoena to appear before the Senate Committee on Labor Racketeering.

Wolfe takes a double shot of scotch, neat. He was acquainted with Longy as a coin man and a *landsman*. There is no way Longy committed suicide. Someone was afraid he would talk to the committee.

> *INTERNATIONAL GANG BELIEVED*
> *INVOLVED IN $10 MILLION THEFT*
> (AP—March 4, 1959) Police raids in Switzerland, Miami, Montreal, New York and Quebec City have turned up over $792,000 in stolen Canadian securities.

William W. Rabin, who called himself a business counselor, was arrested by the FBI as he stepped off a plane at Chicago. He was booked on charges of receiving $98,000 worth of Brockville bonds. The FBI said Rabin got cash for the pledged securities in Paris and Switzerland.[13]

Chicago, March 4, 1959

Trudy thinks he is in New York. Cotroni thinks he is in Switzerland. Mannarino wants to talk. The FBI wants to restrict his movement. A naked lightbulb hangs over the bed in a dingy hotel room. Good place to lay low.

A bellboy knocks on the door. Telegram for Lieutenant Emerson. Unshaven and half undressed, Wolfe opens the door, extends a hand for the telegram. Reaches into his pocket for a tip but comes up empty. The bellboy asks for a signature, but Wolfe waves him off, closes the door.

The telegram is from Rosden in Düsseldorf.

"New available institution too large with four-million-dollar capital. Stop. Suggest known firm owner New York. Signed, Eric."[14]

Require immediate transfer of funds. Wolfe holds the flimsy to the tip of his cigar, watches it consumed in flames, ashes falling into the wastebasket.

Pittsburgh, March 19, 1959

A law enforcement task force comprised of the FBI, the Border Patrol, and state and local police from several states weaves together the evidence in the gun-smuggling investigation. The M1 rifles seized on the Beechcraft C-18 at Morgantown were wrapped in burlap seed bags. The bags had been purchased at the Arnold Cash Feed Store by one of Victor Carlucci's gang. Daniel "Speedo" Hanna drove the truck that delivered the guns. The truck was registered to a company owned by Sam Mannarino. Joe Merola flew the plane up to Pennsylvania from Florida. Stuart Sutor flew the plane with the guns. The plane marked Transit Flasher Company was rented by Norman Rothman. Rothman had strong connections to the casinos in Cuba. So did Mannarino.

Sam Mannarino is subpoenaed to testify before the grand jury. Wearing dark glasses, Sam shields his face from the cameras with a handkerchief. Waiting to be called, he slides a chair into a coat closet, sits with his back to the cameras.

Mannarino's longtime lawyer Charles Margiotti had passed away in 1956. Margiotti's law partner Vincent Casey is now the family's mouthpiece. He accompanies his client to a meeting with the district attorney where they cut a deal. Avoiding reporters, they leave the building down the back stairs. Emerging from the office, the district attorney tells the gathered newshounds, "For reasons we believe are in the best interests of the Government, we have excused Mr. Mannarino at this time."[15]

Speedo Hanna, the driver, requests an audience with Sam Mannarino at the metal yard. He promises he will keep his mouth shut, but he is afraid to go to prison.

Mannarino assures him it will never get to that. "Because we will make arrangements," he tells Speedo, "we will get the case fixed. And if for some unforeseen reason you would be convicted, you will be paid for every day you are on the inside."[16]

Chicago, March 25, 1959

Guns. Bonds. Planes. Casinos. How does it all connect? The FBI keeps circling back to Wolfe. Agent Ed Kinzer calls him for an interview. From the files of the FBI:

> Rabin stated that other than pledging the Canadian Government bonds at the Central National Bank in Chicago and at Switzerland, he never tried to interest any other business institution or individual in the purchasing, pledging, or other handling of any of these bonds. . . . Rabin stated that the purpose of his trips to Canada was to consult with certain business interests of Kent Tomlinson.[17]

New Kensington, Pennsylvania, April 9, 1959

Norman Rothman runs the table against Victor Carlucci in a game of eight ball. But the big man's luck is about to run out. Two men approach the table, flash FBI badges. Rothman, menacing, grips his cue as though to swing it as a bat. The din in Triangle Billiards quickly quiets. Players at other tables melt away. Agents reach for their weapons. Rothman relaxes, drops the cue. Must be a mistake, fellas.

Rothman is arrested and charged with violating the National Stolen Property Act and the National Firearms Act.

Victor Carlucci, Daniel "Speedo" Hanna, Joe Merola, and Stuart Sutor are arrested and charged with conspiracy to transport and export firearms stolen from the U.S. government. Sam Mannarino remains an unindicted coconspirator. Norman Rothman is released on payment of $50,000 bail.

CHAPTER NINE

Biggest Burglary Solved

DRUGS

Montreal, April 28, 1959

PEP COTRONI KNOWS THIS GUY, EDDIE SMITH, NICE GUY, RUNS ERRANDS across the border for him. Encounters him one night at the Club Metropole, a strip joint Cotroni owns with his brothers. Eddie introduces his friend Dave Costa, dark, Italian, wears Ray-Bans indoors. Their meeting was secretly recorded,[1] yielding this exchange:

> Cotroni: Why did you come to see me?
>
> Costa: We heard you're involved in a lot of rackets. Maybe you can help us.
>
> Cotroni: You ever deal in junk?

Pep Cotroni and his brothers Vic and Frank are the biggest heroin dealers in North America. They smuggle high-grade heroin from Corsica to Montreal, where entry is assured by payoffs to dockworkers and customs officers on the take.

Costa offers to make a small buy. Cotroni acts insulted, tells him to come back when he is serious. With cash. The terms of business are cash.

> Cotroni: Although there will be times you will have some good customers, and these are customers you can't let down. Either they will not have the cash, or they will need the narcotics, and you will

have to learn how to feel them out. When you get to know them, you will know which ones to trust and which ones not to trust.

But it is Cotroni's trust that is misplaced. Costa, an alias, is an agent for the Bureau of Narcotics, and he is wearing a wire.

Pep confides to Costa that he is afraid Eddie Smith has got a big mouth.

Cotroni: You know that in this business you can't talk. I like you. You are quiet. You don't make anybody know your business. You know what the score is as far as narcotics go.

The sting plays out over six weeks. Samples are exchanged. Payments confirmed. Good faith demonstrated, honor among thieves. In a car at the Bonfire restaurant, the undercover agent passes Cotroni an envelope with $28,000. Cotroni's trusted gofer René Savard takes Smith and Costa to a warehouse where he gives them four kilos of heroin in neatly sealed packets.

While the drug deal goes down in Montreal, the FBI's investigation of the bonds case intensifies in Chicago.

Agent Malone brandishes a court order at the Central Bank's loan officer Frank Pepe, who protests before opening the vault at Malone's insistence. Malone enters the chamber lined with rows of gleaming steel boxes. He drills into the lock on the box registered to William W. Rabin. The drill spins, emitting tiny shrapnel. Sparks fly. Finally, the lock drops out. But there is a second lock, as on all safety deposit boxes.

Malone drills through the second lock, opens the door, and removes the box. The box is empty. Malone, puzzled, disappointed. Writes in his notebook.

Miami, April 30, 1959

One player who figures in both the Canadian bonds scam and the theft at the armory is Joe Merola. He stays at the Mount Royal while Wolfe, Tomlinson, and Mannarino are in Montreal. He stays at the Warwick same time as Wolfe. More than coincidental to the FBI.

Merola volunteered confidentially that he is deeply in debt and, thus, a possible attraction to him might be a suggestion that a reward of $25,000 has been offered for information leading to the arrest and conviction of the person or persons guilty of captioned theft and the recovery of these bonds. This reward was referred to in previous communication and is offered by the Brockville Trust and Savings Company.[2]

HIDEAWAY
Miami, May 1959

Wolfe alights from a taxi in front of a modest Miami Beach bungalow. He walks up the sidewalk with a spring in his step, knocks on the door. Dollye opens the door, surprised and excited. They embrace and kiss. She feels a tug on her dress. It's her son Jeff, age three. Wolfe notes that the child is wearing braces on his legs. He scoops him up in his arms.

Jeff: Are you a doctor?

Wolfe: Well, I'm a business doctor.

Dollye: This is your Uncle Wolfe.

Jeff: Will you be staying with us?

Dollye explains that the little boy has rickets, and the doctor recommended that he live in a sunny climate.

"That's my other son, Kent junior." She points to a shy six-year-old who appears in the hallway.

Curled up together in bed later, Dollye tells Wolfe that Kent is off flying on a sales trip to poultry plants in the Midwest, he'll be gone for three months. They have got the house for the summer.[3]

Chicago, May 8, 1959

Agent Ed Kinzer is caught off guard when his phone rings. It's Kent Tomlinson, and he wants to come in. He makes a comprehensive statement, furnishing considerable background. The agent records the interview:

He repudiated earlier statements which tended to shield Rabin's activities in connection with the handling of Canadian bonds. In this statement he indicated that Rabin was aided and abetted in his dealings with stolen Canadian Government bonds by Rothman, Cotroni, Mannarino, and Savard.[4]

According to Tomlinson, a plan was formulated in the fall of 1958 by Rabin, Mannarino, Rothman and Giuseppe Cotroni to transfer some $3,000,000 to a bank in Europe for the purchase of arms and that Rabin was to carry out this objective. This figure was later increased to $10,000,000 and a fee of $250,000 for Rabin.[5]

Miami Beach, May 1959

Dollye shoos her boys inside, closes the front door. Dressed in a bikini covered with a shift, carrying her swim bag, she walks to her car at the curb. An elderly neighbor, Mrs. Rauch, approaches. Noting that Dollye often goes swimming, she offers her backyard pool for the children. Dollye declines, in haste.

Dollye: My friend has a cabana at the club.

Mrs. Rauch: Well, if you ever need a sitter for those boys of yours . . .

The offer dangles. Dollye drives away.

Later that month

Lanky John Lenihan ambles up the walk to Dollye's neighbor's house. He opens his wallet, flashes his FBI badge to Mr. and Mrs. Rauch, a retired couple. He shows them some photographs. They identify the photo of Wolfe as the man who appeared to live at the house but say that generally he was there only on weekends. Mrs. Rauch could not identify Kent Tomlinson's photo.[6]

Miami, June 12–21, 1959

Wolfe greets Trudy at the airport, carrying a large bouquet of flowers for her. The big lug. How could she be mad at him?

Checking in at the Biltmore Terrace, the one-time jukebox tycoon is elegant as always in tropical-weight blazer and linen trousers. Trudy in a muumuu with a floral pattern, her Pekinese in her arms. At forty-nine, her features have softened; she's been drinking too much for too long.

Wolfe and Trudy relax in lounges by a cabana at the pool. Wolfe calls an attendant, orders drinks. Put it on my tab. The Rabins are guests of resort owner Norman Rothman.

He can't get Dollye off his mind. He is relieved when he drops Trudy at the airport for her flight back to Chicago.

Agent John Lenihan drops in at the pool club at the Biltmore Terrace. He seeks out the pool manager, a buff twenty-something, Billy Gorin. He shows the pool man a group of photos of men and women from which he picks shots of Wolfe, Dollye, and Norman Rothman. From the files of the FBI:

> *Gorin identified a photograph of Dollye Tomlinson as a person who was also a guest at the Biltmore Terrace during June, 1959. He does not recall the name that this woman used, but he was introduced to her as Mrs. ——. He said he knows she was not introduced as Mrs. Rabin; however, she was a constant associate of Mr. Rabin around the swimming pool, and she shared the same cabana with Mr. Rabin. Gorin recalled that she had 2 children with her, one about two years of age with bow legs, and the other about seven years of age. Gorin described the woman as age 25, 5'6", slender build, very attractive.*[7]

Helpfully, he points out the cabana where Dollye and Wolfe spent many afternoons.

Miami, July 1, 1959

Two FBI agents approach the registration counter at the Biltmore Terrace, flash their badges. Where can they find Norman Rothman? The Cuban manager tells them Rothman is in his office, sixth floor. Points to the elevators. Reaches under the counter, presses a button three times.

The buzzer rings in the big man's penthouse suite. He takes off out the back door. The agents emerge from the elevator on the sixth floor. Rothman is on his way down the back stairwell. Into the parking garage. Into the arms of two more agents blocking the way.

Same time, a nondescript sedan pulls up at Dollye's rented bungalow. Agent Lenihan unfolds his length from the car.

Inside the house, Wolfe has Jeff in his arms.

"Uncle Wolfe will see you tonight," he says, lowering the boy to the floor. Dollye gives him a peck on the cheek. Just like a married couple.

Out the door and into the arms of agent Lenihan.

Dollye comes to the door.

Wolfe calls out to shut the door, don't let the boys see.

New Kensington, Pennsylvania, same time, FBI vehicles surround the scrapyard at the Ken Iron and Steel Company. Sam Mannarino hides in the piles of salvage but is flushed out by agents with an arrest warrant. He surrenders. "I didn't know if I was going to be hit," he tells the FBI.[8] "It was like something out of *The FBI Story*."

In Washington, D.C., agents Benjamin and Ryan escort the lawyer George Rosden in handcuffs from his office building.

Wolfe Rabin, Norman Rothman, Sam Mannarino, and George Rosden are charged with concealing stolen bonds and pledging stolen securities in a scheme to defraud and obtain money by false pretenses. The FBI claims to have solved "the biggest burglary in the world."[9]

Rothman's lawyer Max Lurie, fifty, is waiting at the federal courthouse in Miami when the agents arrive with first Wolfe and then Rothman in handcuffs. Well known for representing Miami's high rollers, the lawyer smoothly arranges their release on bail.

Wolfe is at the pay phone, talking to the operator.

"Collect from Bill for Milton at number 74 in Morden, Manitoba," he says. "No, that is the number, just 74, they don't have dial phones up there."

Milton answers the phone in the store, accepts the charges.

Wolfe is urgent. He is in a jam. He needs $5,000 bail. There's been a mistake, he'll get it cleared up. Can Milt wire the money?

Of course. Family comes first.

Figure 9.1. Collage of headlines. "World's Biggest Burglary Solved." Front pages across America carried a version of this headline reporting the arrest of William Rabin, Sam Mannarino, and Norman Rothman in connection with the bonds stolen from Brockville Trust and Savings. PUBLIC DOMAIN,

Montreal, July 7, 1959

Days after Wolfe is arrested in Miami, RCMP officers in Montreal shadow the American undercover narc "Costa" to an assignation with Pep Cotroni and his cohort René Savard at the import/export warehouse. On the exchange of money and drugs, the agent shows his badge, and the squad moves in, guns drawn. The Canadians take credit for the bust since the U.S. Bureau of Narcotics is out of its jurisdiction.

The feds tear apart Cotroni's clubs, his restaurants, his importing business. Searching for narcotics, they uncover an unexpected bonus: millions of dollars in Government of Canada bonds. Matching bonds on the list stolen from the Brockville Savings and Trust.

The high-profile case against Cotroni for international narcotics trafficking goes to trial three months later. But at the last minute, the key witness refuses to appear. Drug courier turned informant Eddie Lawton Smith fears for his life if he testifies in Montreal. When the court offers to hear Smith in closed session in New York, Pep Cotroni unexpectedly changes his plea to guilty.

Corporal punishment is still legal in Canada in 1959 though rarely used. But in Cotroni's case, the prosecutor calls for the maximum sentence, fourteen years and the lash. "The death penalty is prescribed for a killer. The man who traffics in narcotics is not only a killer but a murderer. His nefarious trade takes the lives, not only of hundreds of addicts, but breaks their families' lives as well."[10]

The judge spares Cotroni a whipping but sentences him to ten years in prison.[11] His accomplice Rene Savard gets a seven-year sentence.

The smack trader's incarceration is a relief for Wolfe. Cotroni won't talk, and the mobster from Montreal won't be coming around to collect for the bonds he fronted Wolfe on consignment.

At the time of Cotroni's conviction, law enforcement agencies around the planet are investigating a host of apparently unrelated criminal activities, including drug trafficking, money laundering, and arms smuggling. The network of associations linking the bank blast in Brockville, the arms theft in Ohio, and the trade in bearer bonds run by Wolfe will prove difficult to establish.

St. Petersburg, Florida, July 18, 1959

Active while he is out on bail, the pilot Stuart Sutor is arrested a second time by U.S. Customs agents at Pinellas Airport as he is loading a B-25 aircraft with spare parts. Sutor had flown the bomber from Tucson, Arizona, to Miami.[12]

Pittsburgh, July 21, 1959

Sam Mannarino meets with Harry Savage in the lobby of the Carlton House. Mannarino tells the lawyer that he had been talking with Vincent Casey and Max Lurie about Rabin's situation, and they felt that the government had a very weak case against Rabin. Mannarino is worried about being charged with aiding and abetting Rabin in disposing of stolen bonds, which he emphasizes he knew nothing about.

Mannarino asks Savage if he would use his position as assistant district attorney to find out what type of evidence the FBI has been able to develop against him.

Nervous, Savage balks. It could be difficult.

Mannarino tells him his fee will be $500 per day as an unofficial consultant to the defense team when Mannarino, Rabin, and Rothman go on trial in Chicago for disposing of the Canadian bonds.

"Rabin's got a Jew lawyer in Chicago. Go see him," he instructs.

Chicago July 25, 1959

Savage goes to the fortieth-floor Miracle Mile office of Joe Green to sound him out on the defense strategy.

The lawyer has bought into Wolfe's story that the bonds came from a Cuban agent named Alfredo Garcia. Based on Wolfe's narrative, the defense will contend that Rabin, by accepting the bonds from Garcia, became, in legalese, a holder in due course. The defense line will be that Rabin accepted the bonds in good faith and thereafter pledged them as collateral for loans.

Green emphasizes to Savage that he has a great deal of respect for the Cook County prosecutor and is "especially worried about a situation in Cook County that usually results in two or three Negros being included as members of the jury. The Negro citizens of Cook County worship the

D.A. and might bring in a conviction for him irrespective of the evidence brought out by the defense."[13]

Back at his office at the Law & Finance Building in Pittsburgh, Savage picks up the phone, dials the FBI.[14] After requesting that his identity be protected, Savage details his meeting with Sam Mannarino.

Pittsburgh, September 13, 1959

An informant calls the FBI to report a conversation he overheard between Sam Mannarino and Norman Rothman. The pair are desperate to find out who appeared in Chicago before the grand jury that had authorized their arrests in the bonds case.[15]

Miami, October 13, 1959

FBI agent John Lenihan sits on a bar stool in the Sea Gull hotel, deep in conversation with an attractive brunette in her thirties who's wearing too much makeup and cheap perfume. Louise Levine is Sam Mannarino's hooker. Lenihan offers her a cigarette, lights it for her.

She tells him that Mannarino would have a date with her about every second or third day he was in town. The dates would usually go to 1:00 a.m., and they would make love. But most of the time, they would sit on the sofa and watch television in his hotel room.

Sam was extremely nervous and jittery, she recalls, and he always wanted to be alone with her. The only time there were other men around was on Christmas Eve.

"And when I got there," she relates, "he told me he had visitors and wouldn't be able to have a date that night. I was pissed because I needed the money, so I didn't pay any attention to the other wise guys."

Lenihan shows her photos of Wolfe, Pep Cotroni, Norman Rothman, and Sam Mannarino, who is the only one she recognizes.

"But he told me his name was Sam Mariano."[16]

Miami, October 1959

An International Harvester station wagon arrives in front of Dollye's rented bungalow. Kent gets out, lumbers up the walk.

Dollye and the boys are sitting on the front step, surrounded by suitcases and boxes. Kent has bought a house on Coronado in the Keys. Full of enthusiasm, he's come to take them to their new home. The boys are excited at the sight of their father. Dollye flashes him a radiant smile. She looks inside wistfully, closes the door to the bungalow behind her.

Miami, December 1959

Deposed Cuban President Fulgencio Batista and his ninety-person entourage take up residence in a wing of the Biltmore Terrace. In the shifting alliances between the underworld and Cuban politicians, Rothman realizes his error in judgment sending arms to the revolutionaries. But his new guests' welfare is not the Capper's top priority. His trial on gunrunning charges is about to begin.

I SMELL A RAT

Pittsburgh, January 11, 1960

Norman Rothman, Victor Carlucci, the pilots Joe Merola and Stuart Sutor, and the driver Daniel "Speedo" Hanna go on trial in federal court in Pittsburgh for crimes and conspiracy in connection with the possession, receiving, transportation, and exportation of firearms stolen from the U.S. government.

Sam Mannarino's new consigliere Vincent Casey defends the racketeer's son-in-law Victor and the surfer-pilot Sutor. Rothman imports Max Lurie from Miami to represent him and the mercenary Merola.

Newspapers headline stories about the Pennsylvania mobsters running guns to Cuba to protect their gambling interests. Wire services feed lurid updates as details of the conspiracy are revealed in court.

The defense lawyers express outrage that the media exposure has prejudiced the jury. They call for a mistrial. When the judge questions the jury members, seven acknowledge having "glanced at" the stories without reading them.[17] But the judge orders the trial to continue.

Pittsburgh, February 4, 1960

On a frigid February day, the verdicts come down: Guilty. Guilty. Guilty. Guilty. Sam Mannarino, not charged in the case, smells a rat. Named Joe

Merola. At a clandestine meeting with an FBI agent, he accuses Rothman's henchman of being a snitch.

> Mannarino: Thirty days after Merola gets outta the joint, he will be murdered. It would be one of those persons, who probably committed some crime with Merola, who would wonder when Merola was going to testify against them. It's gonna be one of these former associates who's gonna kill him.

Mannarino explains why he is talking to the feds. "I want the record to show that I was not going to kill Merola and would have nothing to do with his murder."[18]

Carlucci, Speedo, and the pilots are released on bail pending appeal. Rothman remains behind bars. The district attorney informs Rothman that the attorney general wants to meet with him to discuss a matter of national security. Rothman refuses to go to Washington unless all the other defendants accompany him.[19] Reluctantly, the district attorney releases him.

He is immediately rearrested on conspiracy charges in the Brockville bonds case, to be tried in Chicago. Released on payment of $50,000 bail bond, the casino boss is restricted to the boundaries of Dade County, Florida.

New Kensington, Pennsylvania, June 1960

Sam Mannarino and his brother Gabe, aka "Kelly," drive through the Pennsylvania countryside. Oil derricks dot the horizon. The brothers have incorporated the Ken Oil & Gas Company, looking to get in on the natural resources boom.

Sam reminds Gabe of the money they are making selling silica sand from their property near the crossroads. The silica is used in building highways and has become a profitable operation.[20]

Gabe finishes chewing a chocolate turtle, offers his brother a candy from the box. He stammers when he speaks, a childhood habit the gangster has never overcome.

> Gabe: We gotta take care of Rabin.
> Sam: He's a good guy. I've known him for fifteen years.

Gabe: What if he talked?

Sam: He wouldn't talk.

Gabe: But what if he talked?

The question hangs in the air.

Sam nods. He'll call Al Seid to dispose of Rabin.

They arrive at their claim, where a crew is drilling for natural gas. They have already found gas at six sites.

Al Seid, aka Al Zeyd and Al Ross, a husky man in his mid-forties, is being fitted at his tailor, celebrating his release from the federal pen with a new wardrobe. A childhood immigrant from Russia, Al never became a citizen and had been doing time for violating his immigration status by not reporting to the Immigration and Naturalization Service when his green card expired.

Conferring with the tailor, Al selects light fabrics, he's planning a trip to Florida. According to an FBI informant, Seid is "very much in love with his wife, who is a nymphomaniac residing in Miami Beach."[21]

The telephone rings, the tailor answers, it's for Al. He listens, responds in Russian-accented English.

"Yes, boss. I'll take care of it."

An informant reports to the FBI that "Mannarino, Rothman and others may take necessary steps to 'get rid' of Rabin prior to their forthcoming trial on Interstate Transport of Stolen Property and Conspiracy charges, in view of their feeling that with Rabin out of the way, Mannarino and Rothman cannot be successfully prosecuted."[22]

THE $10,000 BILL

Few Americans today would recognize Salmon P. Chase, the sixth chief justice of the United States (1864–1873). As secretary of the treasury in 1861, Chase put his own face on the $10,000 banknote, the largest denomination ever printed for public consumption. The public rarely ever saw one because these bills were used exclusively by banks and the federal government for large financial transactions. The bill remains legal tender today, although there are fewer than 350 still in existence.

Like a producer casting a movie, Kelly Mannarino calls Wolfe to offer him a role in an imaginative caper involving a million dollars' worth of $10,000 bills.

The banknotes had been stolen during the U.S. occupation of Japan after World War II and smuggled back into the United States. The thief, Mannarino explains to Wolfe, worked for a government agency. On a diplomatic passport, he was above suspicion. But when he sold a few of the $10,000 bills, at a discount, the resulting bank deposit was immediately reported to the Treasury Department, which began an investigation. "As a result of the inquiry," an informant reports to the FBI, "the person in possession of these $10,000 bills has been afraid to sell, spend, or otherwise dispose of them. . . . This person is reportedly still in the U.S. Government service, possibly connected with the United Nations or the State Department."[23]

"We'll get you some fake ID," Kelly tells Wolfe. "You'll get fronted in as a treasury agent. It will scare the shit outta the guy, and he'll hand you the cash. A million bucks! No guns."

Wolfe is reluctant, but he is in dire straits, broke and desperate. Kelly is persuasive.

"You're the only guy with the class to pull this off," he stammers.

Wolfe considers. The shakedown has an elegance that appeals to him. What is the victim going to do, call the FBI?[24]

Miami, August 26, 1960

The Mannarino brothers' hit man Al Seid, who has a contract on Wolfe, drives Wolfe, Joe Merola, and a man identified in the FBI files as "Bernie" to Miami airport. Merola's role is to lead them to the mark. Under assumed names, the three men board an Eastern Airlines flight to Washington, D.C.

Wolfe, Merola, and Bernie get off the plane at a stop in Roanoke, Virginia. Merola tells them he needs to go to Western Union to pick up a wire, they should wait for him. When he returns, he will guide them to the money.

They wait for hours, but Merola never returns. Fed up, Wolfe places a collect call to Al Seid. That little dirtbag Merola has dumped them in a town they don't know with three dollars in his pocket, Wolfe complains. Al Seid wires cash for tickets home.

CHAPTER TEN

Wheels of Justice

Chicago, August 1960

Unable to document Wolfe's story about receiving the bonds from the Cuban agent Garcia, Joe Green drops the case. Wolfe turns to Richard Gorman, forty-six, square-shouldered and square-jawed, looks like a cop, which he had been. Gorman worked the beat while he studied law. On graduating, he was hired by the district attorney's office, where he observed that defending criminals is far more lucrative than prosecuting them. He built a clientele of crime syndicate figures and was considered an expert on finding legal loopholes. He once freed a client in a tax evasion case by arguing that the $900,000 in question was embezzled from the Laundry Workers Union and was therefore not taxable income.[1]

In the summer of 1960, Gorman is in the headlines defending Teamsters Union president James Earl Hoffa, charged with using interstate mail and wires to promote a fraudulent Florida land development scheme. Gorman himself has just been indicted on charges of conspiracy to bribe a juror in a hijacking case.[2] A government witness testifies that Gorman had coached him to lie and rehearsed the perjury with him.[3] Ironically, the judge comes to Gorman's defense as a character witness.

The lawyer assures Wolfe that he will do whatever it takes to keep his clients out of prison. He enters pleas of not guilty to all charges against Wolfe.

His opponent in Wolfe's trial will be a neophyte out to establish himself as a prosecutor. Donald Manion is a decorated veteran of the Korean War. After four years in the navy, the fair-haired, blue-eyed Lieutenant Manion went to law school on the GI Bill. Like his opponent, on graduating, he landed a job in the district attorney's office. In a city with a history of judicial corruption, the thirty-year-old prosecutor has a nagging fear that the bonds case has been assigned to him with the expectation that he will lose.

Manion faces a six-month deadline to take the case to a grand jury. The investigation spans countries and continents. The pieces don't always fit. He makes the strategic decision to focus on Rabin, Mannarino, and Rothman. He also indicts the German lawyer Rosden, who could be a weak link among the conspirators. Manion decides not to press charges against Cotroni and Savard because they are already incarcerated in Quebec.

Miami, September 1960

Rothman drinks with a CIA agent at the bar in a beachfront resort crowded with Cuban exiles. "I love the Cubans," Rothman proclaims. He loves Cuba. But he hates Castro. "He's got my wife, and he won't let her leave."

"Maybe he's doing you a favor," the agent mutters.

Rothman: Whaddya mean?

Agent: Well, you know, it could get a little crowded around the house with Ethel . . .

Rothman: Shut up, motherfucker.

Rothman leans forward, confidentially shares his plan to take out Castro. Before he spreads communism all over South America.

Rothman: I'm an American. My interests are the same as the Government's.[4]

The CIA never follows up on Rothman's scheme to assassinate Castro. The agency has plots of its own to liquidate the revolutionary leader.[5]

Castro tightens his grip on the casinos. As they close down, the new Cuban government expropriates the resorts and shutters the gambling operations. The mob is out hundreds of millions of dollars, and Cuba is off-limits to Americans.

Chicago, October 7, 1960

Castro nationalizes American businesses, including banks, oil refineries, and sugar and coffee plantations. In the United States, policy toward Cuba becomes a major bone of contention in the presidential election. The Democratic candidate, Senator John F. Kennedy, attacks the Republican record on America's closest Caribbean neighbor in a series of televised debates that bring the candidates into the American living room for the first time. Kennedy jabs with his finger and his words, "Mr. Nixon praised the competence and stability of the Batista dictatorship. That dictatorship had killed over 20,000 Cubans in seven years."

The television camera cuts to Kennedy's opponent, Vice President Richard Nixon, a five o'clock shadow, perspiration on his face under the television lights.

Kennedy continues, "We never used our influence, and today Cuba is lost for freedom. I have seen Cuba go to the communists, I have seen communist influence and Castro influence rise in Latin America."[6]

Trudy: Kennedy is like a movie star. And the way he talks—

Wolfe: —phony patrician—

Trudy: Don't you think he would make a good president?

Wolfe: That cocksucker Kennedy! And his pissant little brother. They think they're better than the rest of us. Their old man was importing booze from the Bronfmans, back in the day. What is he gonna do about Castro? Send in the marines to recover the casinos for Lansky?

Miami, November–December 1960

Focused on his legal defense, unbeknownst to Wolfe, his very life is in a precarious position.

In Rothman's office at the Biltmore Terrace, the Mannarino brothers' main man in Miami asks hit man Al Seid why he hasn't disposed of Rabin yet.

Al pauses. "I haven't seen him around."

Rothman: The boys want you to get rid of Rabin.

Al: I haven't decided if I'm gonna handle the job personally. I might wanna subcontract this one.[7]

Rothman: You like the guy. I do too. He's a *mensch*.

Al: Business is business.

Fortunately for Wolfe, the Mannarinos lose interest while Al Seid stalls. An informant reports to the FBI that "the outfit [the Mannarino group] has ceased efforts to locate and 'take care of' Bill Rabin. Rothman and others are now exerting considerable efforts to identify two unknown witnesses from the Miami area who testified before the Federal Grand Jury in Chicago which indicted Rothman, Mannarino, and others."[8]

Miami, February 8, 1961

The CIA is approached by Joe Merola, who "expressed interest in offering his assistance in connection with the Cuban situation." The CIA report notes that Merola is at liberty on "an appeal being taken against a conviction involving a theft of guns from a National Guard Armory. Merola was given five years, but his appeal is expected to drag on indefinitely."[9]

Bay of Pigs, Cuba, April 17, 1961

More than 1,400 paramilitary troops funded by the CIA land on the beach in the Bay of Pigs on the southwest coast of Cuba. But when President John F. Kennedy withdraws the air support of CIA-supplied B-26 bombers, the invading force is quickly defeated by troops loyal to Fidel Castro and the revolution, and the invaders surrender. The failed invasion becomes a signature defeat for U.S. foreign policy.

Chicago, April 18, 1961

The telephone rings in Wolfe's room at the Emerson. Wolfe grabs for the call. A smile breaks out across his face. His lawyer has good news. The judge assigned to the case has resigned. The hearing is continued indefinitely. The wheels of justice grind slowly. But not slowly enough for Norman Rothman, Joe Merola, Stuart Sutor, and Victor Carlucci.

Chicago, April–May 1961

Special agent Ed Kinzer Jr. burns the midnight oil at the FBI's Chicago office, pounding away on his Remington. He has been tasked with writing the complaint in the bonds investigation. A detective with a law degree, he approaches the assignment by creating a narrative attempting to weave the multiple strands of the investigation into a convincing case.

He draws on the reports from agents in the Chicago, Pittsburgh, and Miami field offices, compiling the evidence available to prove the theft of an estimated $14 million in bonds. He writes chapters on the evidence against Wolfe, Sam Mannarino, Norman Rothman, and the fixer George Rosden.

Kinzer stubs out a cigarette into an overflowing ashtray. He rolls a sheet of paper out of the carriage. He's done. The fifty-eight-page report, dated May 10, 1961, is sent to J. Edgar Hoover, director of the FBI in Washington, D.C.

The status of Kinzer's report is changed to unclassified in 1985, but it is not released. The report is reviewed and redacted in 1998. It is finally released under the John F. Kennedy Assassination Records Collection Act in 2017.

Leechburg, Pennsylvania, June 24, 1961

Sam Mannarino's restaurant, the Bonfire, has the same name as Pep Cotroni's drive-in café in Montreal. Sam is proud of the cuisine and enjoys playing host. A waiter serves the brothers veal parmesan and fettucine from their mother's recipe. He pours from a bottle of Valpolicella and hangs around.

Sam and Gabe are worried about the imminent incarceration of the group convicted in the National Guard Armory case. While they are free on bond for eighteen months, an appeals court upholds the convictions, and then the Supreme Court refuses to hear the case. The Mannarino brothers' discussion is reported to the FBI by the waiter:

> *Sam Mannarino said it was a real blow to lose Norman Rothman, who is a top-flight Cuban contact man; Red Giordano, who is a first-rate fence, and even Speedo Hanna, who is very efficient as a gambling dealer and strong-arm enforcer. Mannarino said the loss of these men would create some hard-to-fill openings.*[10]

Miami, July 10, 1961

Wolfe drives Rothman's white Cadillac convertible, a twenty-two-foot-long finned land yacht, to the Bel Aire Hotel, where Rothman's sons Cappy and Sandy are running the bar. Under the terms of his parole for the National Guard Armory case, the Capper himself is not permitted to drive.

Entering the hotel, Rothman strikes up a conversation with FBI agent John Lenihan, who, purely by coincidence, is just leaving after an appointment on an unrelated investigation. Wolfe recognizes Lenihan, the agent who arrested him outside Dollye's house. Their eyes meet.

Lenihan: Nothing personal. Just doing my job.
Wolfe: That's what all the Nazis say.

Beat. He extends his hand. They shake.

Lenihan: You still shacked up with that Tomlinson babe?
Wolfe: Nah. Her husband's back in town.

In an affable mood, Rothman tells Lenihan that he has been in Washington, D.C., where he spoke to "big people" in connection with his case. The agent reports Rothman's optimism that he probably won't have to serve time on the gunrunning conviction in Pittsburgh.

The conversation is interrupted by a page over the hotel loudspeaker. Telephone call for Sam Mannarino.

Rothman picks up a lobby phone, calls the switchboard operator, cups his hand over the phone. Lenihan strains to listen but can't make out the conversation.[11]

Miami, August 14, 1961

Desperate to avoid his pending prison term, Joe Merola contacts the FBI. Agents Tom Forsyth and John Portella fly to Miami from Pittsburgh to conduct the interview. Merola insists that lawyers from the Department of Justice also be present.

Meeting at the Federal Building, Merola sets the conditions: that he will never testify to any information furnished and that his identity will be protected so that none of his information could ever be traced back to him.

Merola dishes out all the dirt he can dig up on the Mannarino syndicate. Sam, he tells the agents, is "a real nut, who falls for all sorts of crazy schemes. He's always ready to listen to any kind of a business deal, and he almost always ends up as the patsy since the deals are rarely successful."[12]

Norman Rothman, according to Merola, steals from the Mannarinos; even when they lose, he comes out with cash. "He's full of shit about Cuba, and when something really needs to get done, he calls me."

Al Seid has a reputation as an enforcer, but there's actually only one guy he disposed of, and that was in Cleveland.

At the conclusion of the interview, Merola advises the agents that he is scheduled to surrender to a U.S. marshal in Pittsburgh to begin serving his sentences. If the agents will meet him there one day prior, Merola tells them he is certain he will have by then recalled additional information of value to the FBI and would be willing to talk without the Department of Justice attorneys present.[13]

But the meeting never takes place, and Merola never turns himself in to the marshal. Later, he brags that he won't have to do any time. He tells an FBI informant that his case has been taken care of in Philadelphia and that it has cost him a "tremendous bundle" to have his pending five-year sentence suspended and be placed on probation.[14]

Surfside, Florida, August 28, 1961

A Bureau of Prisons van idles in the drive at Rothman's villa, belching exhaust. Armed guards escort the big man in manacles to the van. Through the grated window, Rothman watches the gates of his mansion and his freedom recede from view. Eight bumpy hours on a wooden seat later, the van arrives in Atlanta and transfers him to the United States Penitentiary to serve his sentence for gunrunning.

Chicago, October 18, 1961

On a brisk autumn morning, Wolfe and his lawyer Richard Gorman climb the steps to the Federal Building. For more than two years since his arrest in Miami, Wolfe has been at liberty, suffering only the annoyance of an occasional court appearance. But the postponements are coming to an end. A new judge has the case on his docket.

Entering the courtroom, Wolfe banters with Sam Mannarino. They pass George Rosden at his table, stone-faced. The German gestures to Wolfe.

Rosden: Your fly is open.

Wolfe shoots him a look.

Wolfe: Only a cocksucker would notice a thing like that!

Mannarino snorts.

Laughter stops at the entrance of Judge Joseph Sam Perry, sixty-six, a grumpy, independent-minded former Democratic state politician appointed to the bench in 1951 by President Harry Truman.

The hearing is called to set a trial date. Through black-rimmed glasses, Judge Perry looks over the defendants. Wolfe. Mannarino. The German, Rosden. Three. He frowns. Where is the fourth defendant, Rothman?

Manion informs the court that Rothman is in prison in Atlanta for gunrunning. The judge reminds him that the court can't proceed without all defendants present. Embarrassed, Manion asks for a writ of habeas corpus to permit Rothman to be transported to Chicago.

Escorted by Bureau of Prisons guards, Rothman appears in Judge Perry's court two weeks later. He punches Wolfe lightly on the shoulder in passing. Hang tough, *boychik*. With all defendants present, the judge calendars the trial to commence January 15, 1962.

Montana, November 1961

Deep in the Montana woods, Sam Mannarino and another hunter are stalking an elk. Rangers approach. Sam shows his hunting license, but that is not the problem. The ranger has a warrant; Sam is wanted for violating his terms of bail by leaving Pennsylvania without the court's permission.

I'm under police supervision, Mannarino explains. He introduces his "buddy," Officer Al Hanna of the New Kensington, Pennsylvania, police. His brother Speedo had been convicted in the gunrunning case.

"He is in my custody," officer Hanna protests.

"You can tell it to the judge," the ranger tells them, "when he gets back on Monday."

Miami, December 27, 1961

Assistant district attorney Don Manion arrives in Miami on the red-eye from Chicago. Jealous colleagues jibe he is using the case to take a Florida vacation. Manion has forty-eight hours to present the bonds case to the grand jury, or the indictments will lapse. Despite the extent of the investigation, he is uncertain. He hopes to find the missing pieces to the puzzle here, in the Florida humidity.

Manion tracks down Kent Tomlinson, whose FBI file is full of intriguing references. He suspects Tomlinson was running bonds from Canada with Rabin. He taxis to a Florida mid-mod on Coronado Drive, where he walks to the entrance, an out-of-place wool suit from Chicago, fumbling for his notebook. Knocks on a bungalow door. A willowy brunette in halter and pedal pushers—Dollye—responds. Kent? Who wants him?

Kent appears, an eight-year-old boy in tow. He allows Manion to enter but refuses to answer questions without his lawyer.

Manion sweats in the humidity, waiting. Max Lurie, last seen in Pittsburgh defending Rothman in the gunrunning case, arrives in a crisp seersucker suit. He advises Manion to save his time, his client will be taking the Fifth Amendment. As the prosecutor waits for a taxi, the question occurs to Manion, how did this two-bit con man in the burbs get a connected lawyer on call?

It never occurs to Manion to interview Dollye, Tomlinson's beauty-queen wife.

Lying awake at 1:00 a.m. in his hotel room, Manion churns the case in his mind. Interrupted by telephone rings. FBI calling. Tomlinson told the FBI he wants to meet with the prosecutor, alone. Manion hopes the con man wants to cut a deal.

Manion taxis to an office building, finds the suite, a dentist's office. Lights out, but the door opens. Tomlinson, in the chair, speaks from the shadows.

> Tomlinson: I'm not going to testify. I'm the only friend Wolfe Rabin's got.
>
> Manion: Your friend got in over his head.
>
> Tomlinson: Wolfe is telling the truth!
>
> Manion: Come clean with me. Did you get the bonds when you went to Montreal with Rabin?
>
> Tomlinson: Look, Wolfe is coming over on Saturday. I'm going to get things straightened out and I'll call you back and let you know.[15]

Manion threatens to issue an indictment with Tomlinson's name on it if he doesn't hear back that the pilot is going to testify.

Chicago, December 29, 1961

The grand jury is among the most secret institutions of the American system of justice. Twenty-three citizens must weigh the district attorney's accusations to decide if the state will go to the expense of trial. On the Friday before New Year's Eve, the December 1961 group of jurors is anxious to complete its month of civic duty.

For Don Manion, it is the eleventh hour. The indictments have been on the books for two and a half years and will expire if he can't convince the grand jury to go to trial.

Manion weaves a far-flung tale of conspiracy and money laundering. He charges that Wolfe devised a scheme to defraud and to obtain money and property by means of false and fraudulent pretenses. Wolfe made representations and promises. He boasted that he was going to buy a bank.

The prosecutor's narrative begins with the $14 million in bonds stolen from Brockville Trust. Rabin, he charges, converted and sought to convert the bonds into money and credit by pledging them as security for loans and investing them with banks in the United States and Europe. He enters into evidence the nine $1,000 Canada bonds with charred edges the FBI found in Wolfe's desk.

Following Wolfe's travels across Europe, Cuba, Canada, and the United States, he unfolds a variety of ploys acted out to pledge more than $100,000 in securities. The conspirators, he charges, knew the bonds to have been stolen and transported in interstate and foreign commerce.

The grand jury members demand to see evidence of the conspiracy. Manion presents hotel registers, airline manifests, telephone and telegraph registers to place the conspirators together.

"Just like that movie *Ocean's Eleven*," a juror mutters. "The one with Frank Sinatra, Dean Martin, and Sammy Davis Junior." "And don't forget Joey Bishop. The whole Rat Pack."

The grand jury finds Manion's narrative compelling. The jury votes to proceed to trial.

January 2, 1962
New arrest warrants are issued by the U.S. Marshals Service for William Rabin, Sam Mannarino, Norman Rothman, and George Rosden.

CHAPTER ELEVEN

Scheme and Artifice

MANEUVERS
Chicago, January 5, 1962

BELOW-ZERO TEMPERATURES HAVE KEPT CHICAGO IN A DEEP FREEZE for days without relief. The winds gusting off Lake Michigan, the icy streets, and snow-covered vehicles take Wolfe's thoughts back to the harsh winters growing up in Manitoba, the good times with his brothers and sisters. Scoring a goal for the family hockey team. Playing the sax in his band Wolfe Rabinovitch & the White Caps. Running booze into North Dakota in a blizzard.

A platoon of men in overcoats, hats, and scarves climbs the slippery steps to the Federal Building. Trudy, in a mink coat, steadies herself on Wolfe's arm. She looks up at the Beaux Arts dome, concerned and fearful.

Wolfe is accompanied by his lawyer, Richard Gorman, the ex-cop with inventive methods of convincing juries. Vincent Casey has flown in from Pittsburgh to represent Sam Mannarino.

Norman Rothman engages a Chicago celebrity lawyer, Bradley Eben, who appears as the judge on the WGN-TV weekly drama *They Stand Accused*.[1] Eben is an ironic choice of representation. In 1950, he had been staff counsel for Senator Estes Kefauver's committee investigating organized crime in interstate commerce and later a campaign manager for the crime-busting senator's presidential candidacy in the Democratic primaries in 1952 and 1956.

Outside the courtroom, a reporter catches sight of Trudy. Look, it's the blonde. The herd surrounds Wolfe and Trudy.

Reporter: Are you his secretary?
Trudy: I'm Mrs. Rabin.

A photographer takes her picture. Wolfe raises a hand to shield his face. Trudy summons her bravado.

Trudy: I've never been to an arraignment. Wouldn't miss it for the world.

Like a fullback, Gorman shoves through the throng, shepherds her down the corridor to room 67, the courtroom presided over by Judge Joseph Sam Perry. All rise on his Honor's entrance.

The grand jury's indictments are read aloud. Wolfe is charged with four felony counts of pledging a total of $98,000 in securities to the Central National Bank as security for a loan, with the knowledge that the bonds had been stolen from the Brockville Trust.

The fifth count charges Wolfe with unlawfully concealing securities, the $9,000 in Dominion of Canada bonds seized from the desk at the Rek Chemical Company.

Counts one through five are the opening acts in an epic narrative of alleged crimes. Wolfe is portrayed in the sixth count as the mastermind of a multinational criminal conspiracy, the architect of a "scheme and artifice" to obtain money and property by defrauding banks and banking institutions in the United States and Europe. Indicted along with Wolfe are Sam Mannarino, Norman Rothman, and George Rosden, who "willfully, knowingly and feloniously did aid, abet, counsel, induce and procure the commission of the felonious offense."

Wolfe and his alleged conspirators are further charged with using wire communications and interstate and foreign commerce to transport stolen securities in the largest money-laundering scheme in history. Nine counts total.

After each count is read, Judge Perry asks the defendants, "How do you plead?" To each charge, a chorus in response: "Not guilty, your Honor."

Chicago, January 20, 1962

Hobbling into the courtroom on a cane, Wolfe shows up with his left foot bandaged, says he broke his toe. Rosden petitions for a separate trial. Denied. Mannarino offers the Fraternal Order of Police lodge a gumball vending machine with the proceeds to go to the police widows' fund.[2] The police fraternity declines Mannarino's generosity.

Judge Sam Perry is fed up with the maneuvering and distractions that are turning his courtroom into a circus before the trial has even begun. Worse, it is seemingly impossible to select a jury. Some prospective jurors say they have read newspaper stories reporting that defendant Rothman is serving a federal prison term for gunrunning. Others answer yes to the question of whether they would be prejudiced against Rothman if there is evidence that he had supported Cuban dictator Fidel Castro, who is a communist. In the first three days, twenty-one citizens are excused for cause, seven on peremptory challenges by the defense, two on challenges by the government.

With eight persons in the jury box, the judge asks if any feel that they would be unduly prejudiced in favor of the prosecution by the testimony of an FBI agent.

All eight raise their hands. The judge, exasperated, bangs his gavel.

Figure 11.1. William Rabin outside courtroom, Chicago, January 17, 1962. COURTESY OF CHICAGO HISTORY MUSEUM STM-037008041, PHOTO BY BOB KOTALIK/*CHICAGO SUN-TIMES*.

Judge Perry: Do you mean to tell me that all of you people would believe a law enforcement officer over anybody else? This is a conspiracy to shirk your duty! I believe you are saying that you are favoring law enforcement testimony just to evade jury duty. I don't think you are being honest![3]

Judge Perry sends the men and women in the box on their way. He limits the defense to three more challenges.

Chicago, January 23, 1962

Judge Perry's head lolls on his shoulder. He snores.

Wolfe (to Gorman): I can't believe they let the judge fall asleep on the bench.

No one dares to wake him up.

Wolfe glances sideways, sees Mannarino at his table conferring with his lawyer. Tries to catch his eye. Sam's olive complexion is pasty, eyes swollen.

Mannarino doesn't appear in court after the lunch recess. Vincent Casey explains that his client recently suffered two heart attacks and has been taken to the hospital for observation. Skeptical—defendants will use any excuse for delay—Judge Perry orders a court-appointed physician to examine Mannarino to determine whether his illness might require that the trial be postponed.

The doctor reports that Sam has an infected tooth, gingivitis, a coronary condition, and a high fever with the threat of pneumonia.

PROSECUTION
Chicago, February 1, 1962

A jury of seven women and five men is finally confirmed. Before Don Manion can call the government's first witness, the attorneys for three codefendants move for acquittal, asserting that Manion's opening statement outlines a basis of prosecution only against Wolfe, the rest of the government's case is mere guilt by association. Motions denied.[4]

Scheme and artifice. Prologue. Manion opens with photographs of the blasted vault in Brockville—the biggest bank robbery in the world.

He introduces the first witness, a Canadian police officer in crisp blue uniform, bristle moustache, right you are, eh. Sergeant Leslie Sterritt of the Brockville Police recounts the aftermath of the blast at Brockville Trust.

> Sergeant Sterritt: They broke through a bank wall five feet thick and then cut through a vault wall of steel plate with acetylene torches. . . . When I got there, I found traces of smoke still in the premises. . . . There was considerable rubble, bricks, plaster, mortar, and a considerable quantity of documents and Canada Savings Bonds.

Manion makes clear that the men on trial are not charged with robbing the bank. But he intends to prove their guilt in a scheme to launder millions of dollars in bonds that originated in the Brockville Trust vault.

Chicago, February 2, 1962
Brinks guards carry boxes of bonds into the courtroom. Banker Frank Pepe takes the witness stand. He removes stacks of bonds from the boxes to be placed into evidence.

> Manion: Would you read or describe each one of those bonds individually by the issuing authority, the face value, the maturity date, the rate, and the coupons attached, sir?
>
> Gorman interjects: If the court please, there must be some way to shortcut that procedure.
>
> Manion: I wish there were, your Honor, but these are worth $100,000, and I don't want to take custody or put them in evidence here without having a description of the value of these things.

After interminably reading into the record the serial number for each bond, Manion asks Pepe to recount Wolfe's transactions at the bank.

> Pepe: Wolfe told me he was reorganizing or liquidating some company and that he needed some funds. Would I make him a loan? I said, "What security have you got?" And he showed me the bonds. I

said, "How long do you want the loan for?" "Oh, just a short time." And I made him the loan.

Manion: And in the course of the conversations you had on September 16 and September 29, was there any conversation to the source of the bonds?

Gorman: I will object to that as leading the witness.

Judge Perry: It is leading. Objection sustained.

Manion protests. He pleads that he is attempting to show that the bonds that Rabin pledged at the bank came from the Brockville Trust and Savings.

Manion: We expect to show that he pledged some of those bonds in Switzerland, others I am afraid only Mr. Rabin knows what happened to them.

Gorman: I object to that statement in the presence of the jury.

Judge Perry: The comment may be stricken.

Rosden's lawyer cross-examines Frank Pepe, asks the banker if his client's name appears on any of the exhibits. Judge Perry wipes his brow. The defense is entitled to request a repetition of identification of every document. He stares at the district attorney through his black frames. Manion gets the signal. Best to curry favor.

Manion: If the court please, we will stipulate to the fact that Mr. Rosden's name does not appear on any of the exhibits.

The lawyers for Rothman and Mannarino immediately demand the same stipulation.

Judge Perry: So stipulated, that the names of none of the defendants except Rabin appear on those particular records.

Eben: I move to strike all of the testimony of Mr. Pepe on the grounds that it is irrelevant and immaterial insofar as Mr. Rothman is concerned.

Lawyers for Mannarino and Rosden join in the motion.

Judge Perry: The motion is granted.

Wolfe turns to Gorman. They just threw me under the bus. With friends like that . . .

Judge Perry: So the jury understands, so far the only evidence we have had here about loans negotiated is as to defendant Rabin. There hasn't been any evidence so far that would tend to connect the other defendants with this. In order to keep the record straight we will allow this evidence to go against the defendant—

Wolfe: Shit.

Judge Perry: —and then the Government will have the responsibility of moving to admit this evidence against the other defendants when, as, and if evidence is introduced that would warrant you in considering them as coconspirators.

Court recesses. Leon's wife Val encounters Trudy in the ladies' room. Their relationship is still frosty. Val sees that her sister-in-law is pale, muttering "oh my God" over and over.

Val searches through Trudy's purse, comes up with a small pillbox, offers Trudy a tiny pink tablet. Brings her a cup of water. Trudy gulps down the pill, nods her thanks.

COLLOQUY

Gorman objects to the prosecution introducing into evidence the records of Wolfe's safety deposit box. Judge Perry orders the jury to leave the courtroom and the lawyers to approach the bench. The judge wants to know why the prosecution appears to be concerned, not with the contents of the box but with what it doesn't contain.

Manion: We expect our evidence in the course of this trial to show that on January 29, 1959, Rabin withdrew $9,000 in bonds and that instead of putting them in a safety deposit box, which was accessible to him, we expect to show he put them in the drawer of a desk in a warehouse. The point is, sir, Rabin would have $9,000 of bonds, he doesn't cash them, he doesn't put them in a safety deposit box, he puts them in a drawer. His activities in that regard seem to me to be relevant to the man's intent.

Judge Perry: You are seeking to show that he had a safety deposit box available within which to put them?

Manion: Yes, sir.

Judge Perry: But he didn't do it? Is that what you are seeking to show? Is that all you are trying to prove by these different items?

Manion: Yes, sir, really I feel it is relevant—

Rosden's lawyer: If this type of evidence goes to scienter,[5] I would be guilty of something every hour on the hour!

Manion: —it seems to me a little strange to take $9,000 like cash and put it in a desk in a warehouse when you have got a safety deposit box at the same location that—

Rosden's lawyer: I have no right to lodge this objection, except if this type of evidence is permitted to permeate this trial as far as my man is concerned, guilt would be pretty easily established.

Judge Perry makes a nondecision, reserving his ruling on the admissibility of the safety deposit box records until when, as, and if evidence comes in that Rabin put the bonds in an open drawer.

WITNESS
Chicago, February 7, 1962
Travel agent George Hoyt fumbles with his glasses, nervous on the witness stand. Both Wolfe and Tomlinson are in the courtroom, but he is unable to identify them. Prodded by Manion, he tentatively points to a man with a cane and his foot bandaged at the defense table. Satisfactory identification for the impatient judge.

Judge Perry: The record may show that the gentleman who he said might be Mr. Rabin is in fact the defendant Rabin.

Manion questions the travel agent about the itinerary he prepared for Wolfe. Was there an issue over payment for the first-class airline tickets?

Hoyt: When I insisted on cash, Mr. Rabin reached down to his satchel and patted it and said, "Why, we have enough bonds to take care of any obligations."

Mannarino mouths at Wolfe, "Did you really say that?" His lawyer stands to cross-examine Hoyt.

Casey: Mr. Hoyt, you testified yesterday that there were displayed in your office bonds which were described to you in the amount of $200,000 or $300,000?

Hoyt: They were not displayed to see them. They were referred to in a briefcase—

Casey: But your testimony is now that no one ever displayed to you in your office any bonds during the course of the negotiations for the tickets?

Hoyt: I did not see any full view of the bonds.

Casey: That is all.

Judge Perry: The witness is excused.

February 8, 1962

Kent Tomlinson takes the stand, a grim expression on his Florida-tanned face. He warned Manion how he will respond if he is subpoenaed.

Manion: Do you know the defendant William Rabin?

Tomlinson: I refuse to answer on the grounds it may tend to incriminate me.

Manion: Do you know the defendant Norman Rothman?

Tomlinson: I refuse to answer on the grounds it may tend to incriminate me.

Manion: Do you know the defendant Sam Mannarino?

Tomlinson: I refuse to answer on the grounds it may tend to incriminate me.

Manion: Isn't it true, sir, that yesterday you advised me that you were fearful for your safety and that of your wife if you were to testify?

Tomlinson: I refuse to answer on the grounds it may tend to incriminate me.

Manion: Didn't you inform me, sir, that your wife was being harassed by phone calls in the middle of the night in which there were various obscenities?

Eben: Just a moment, your Honor. I am going to interpose an objection to this.

Rothman's showy television lawyer Bradley Eben takes the stage.

Eben: This is not a McClellan Committee; this is not a senatorial quiz. None of these last few questions have anything to do—

Judge Perry: Objection sustained.

February 9, 1962

Next on Manion's list is Joe Merola, sent from the Tallahassee Correctional Institute, where he is serving his sentence for gunrunning. While he waits to take the stand, Mannarino mouths "weasel." Judge Perry frowns.

According to newspaper accounts, Merola's testimony puts Wolfe together with Sam Mannarino and Pep Cotroni in Montreal in September 1958.

But Merola's actual testimony cannot be quoted. What he said under oath has been excised from the transcript of proceedings. Not merely redacted, completely excised. By whom, and why? The record of payments for his services suggests that the pilot's highly placed connections in the CIA had Merola's testimony expunged on grounds of national security.

Weasel

The disparate pieces of the prosecution's case are taking time to unfold. Judge Perry wants to know the direction the case is going. The prosecution and the defense lawyers gather in the judge's chambers.

Manion: Do I understand, your Honor, that if we would place these individuals together within this period of time, would your Honor consider that sufficient foundation?

Judge Perry: Placing them together, mere association is not enough. In the Tomlinson matter you showed him as the recipient of some of the bonds that were received by Rabin. I said that is sufficient to connect him as being an interested party.

Manion: All that I can say, your Honor, is that we expect to show Rabin and Mannarino and Cotroni were associating together within this period of time. The problem we are faced with on the one hand, the mere showing that they are together is not sufficient to establish it, and on the other we can't get in a conversation to color their association. We are on the horns of a dilemma from which we cannot remove ourselves.

Eben: You certainly are. Because the nail could be pulled out, your Honor, but the hole in the wall will show to this jury through all time through this case.

The judge instructs Manion to move it along.

The prosecution calls Eddie Lawton Smith, yet another witness already in custody. Manion presents him as a witness to the conspiracy. He recalls an evening at the Café Montmartre in Manhattan in June 1958.

Smith: We was with two broads from the Copa and then Pep Cotroni came into the bar. I waved to him and he came over, so we caught up.

Then, the informant testifies, Cotroni left to join two men waiting at a table in the back. One of them is in the courtroom. He identifies Sam Mannarino.

The defense attacks the witness's credibility.

Gorman: Have you ever been known by any name other than Edward Lawton Smith?

Smith: Yes, sir.

Gorman: What other names have they been?

Smith: Joe Beard, Eddie O'Hare, Frank Russo, and Joe Franklin.

Eben: You work as an informer?

Smith: No, sir.

Eben: As an undercover man?

Smith: That's right, sir.

Eben: That's what you call yourself?

Smith: That's right. Read the papers.

Eben: You make a distinction between an undercover and an agent?

Smith: One carries a badge and a gun and he maneuvers in the street. I work a different way.

Eben: Did you tell Cotroni at that time that there were some people in New York for whom you were dealing?

Smith: That's correct.

Eben: And you wanted to buy bonds from him?

Smith: They wanted to buy bonds from him.

Eben: So you were soliciting him to sell you bonds.

Smith: Not to sell me bonds, Mr. Eben.

Eben: To sell other people bonds?

Smith: That's right.

Eben: You knew this was a crime?

Smith: That's right.

Eben: You were trying to get Mr. Cotroni to enter into crime with the people represented by you, isn't that right?

Smith: I was trying to make a setup, yes, for the government.

Eben: In other words, you were trying to entrap Mr. Cotroni into this?

The judge points out that Cotroni is not on trial in this case. Simply because he is named as an unindicted coconspirator does not make him guilty, despite his narcotics conviction in Canada.

Gorman grabs for the opening, moves to strike the informant's entire testimony.

> Gorman: It has nothing to do with the conspiracy charged in this indictment, and it certainly does not prove what the United States attorney said that he was going to show, that it was in furtherance of any conspiracy.

The judge agrees and orders Eddie Lawton Smith's testimony stricken from the record.[6] The informer's testimony has already made headlines in the newspapers, but striking it undermines the prosecution's conspiracy case before the jury.

CHAPTER TWELVE

Shoot the Moon

PRECIPICE

Chicago, February 15, 1962

REPORTERS ENCOUNTER WOLFE, DISHEVELED, IN THE FEDERAL Building corridor. His room at the Edison has been robbed.

> Wolfe: The place was ransacked. Somebody rifled through my files.
> Reporter: Are you going to file a complaint?
> Wolfe: What am I going to do, call the FBI? Ask him!

He gestures at Manion approaching, carrying an armload of files.

Court convenes. Sam Mannarino is absent. Vincent Casey rises to explain that his client's father passed away. Judge Perry orders the trial recess for a week.

Pittsburgh, February 23, 1962

The chant of the Ave Maria echoes through the dome of the Basilica of Saints Peter and Paul. Mourners file past the bier for the final viewing of Giorgio Mannarino. Women weep at the coffin. Men smelling of cigars and cologne kiss brothers Sam and Kelly Mannarino on both cheeks, offering condolences.

Father Nicola Fusco officiates at the funeral. The cathedral is packed with representatives of other families come to pay their respects to the

Mannarino patriarch. John LaRocca. Michael Genovese. Lawyer Vincent Casey. The mayor of Pittsburgh. The New Kensington chief of police.

Limousines with a motorcycle police escort deliver the funeral party to the cemetery. FBI agents watch from the perimeter, photographing with long lenses.

February 23, 1962

> *Memorandum*
> *To: Director, FBI*
> *From: SAC, Pittsburg*
> *Assistant District Attorney Manion told Special Agent John Shwartz "it is fully believed that defendant William Rabin will take the stand and implicate his co-defendants, including Samuel Mannarino. . . . It is noted that both Merola and Rabin have been associates and friends of the Mannarinos for many years . . . the testimony of these two men might be a selling point with [name redacted] to demonstrate that others were turning on the Mannarinos to save themselves."[1]*

Had the Mannarinos and Rothman had an accurate instinct when they contracted hitman Al Seid to "dispose of" Wolfe to keep him silent? Would he implicate them if he testified?

Old Chicago Courthouse, February 26, 1962

Manion's assistants unfurl a large map. It has lines connecting Montreal to Chicago, Chicago to Zürich–Basel–Munich–Liechtenstein, Paris to New York, Pittsburgh to Havana. Europe is an abstract expressionist overlay of colored lines. The prosecutor promises the jury that the testimony will unravel the connections.

A succession of Swiss bankers testifies. Herr Vogelsang recalls the defendant Rosden saying that it was difficult for his client Mr. Rabin to find a way to fructify this money.[2] Dr. Siegel testifies that he told Herr Rabin that his bank was definitely not for sale. The Credit Suisse banker complains that the bank has been able to recover only $20,000 of the funds loaned to Mr. Rabin.

Manion brings in a Cuban nightclub operator and an FBI agent with testimony to support his theory that Mannarino and Rothman are casino operators who got Rabin in on the bonds-for-guns-to-Castro deal. The defense objects that the testimony is irrelevant, but it makes sensational headlines.

BROCKVILLE BONDS USED BY CUBANS?
Lawyer Was Told Stolen Bonds Came from Castro Men
Chicago (UPI)—Testimony of an international lawyer has linked supporters of Cuban Premier Fidel Castro with bonds stolen in history's biggest bank burglary.[3]

Manion calls Robert Malone, the FBI agent who has doggedly pursued his investigation of the case for two years. Malone testifies to finding $9,000 in bonds in Wolfe's desk. In his cross-examination, Gorman focuses on Malone's notes of the investigation, which are missing.

Gorman: Can you tell me when you destroyed your notes of this case?
Malone: Immediately after we dictated the interview report form.
Gorman: Can you tell us why you destroyed those notes, Mr. Malone?
Malone: Actually, it is a procedure we have, in order not to make our files too bulky.
Gorman: Did you destroy the notebook because the notes would confirm that the safety deposit box was empty?
Manion: Objection!

Gorman moves to have the witness's testimony stricken. Motion denied.[4]

The district attorney has a final filip. Seeking to provide further evidence of conspiracy, the prosecution's seventieth witness is the bellboy who delivered a telegram from Europe to Wolfe's room at the North Park Hotel.

Bellboy: He said he was Lieutenant Emerson, but he wasn't wearing a uniform.

Manion: What else do you remember?

Bellboy: He reached into his pocket, but he said he didn't have any change for a tip!

Laughter. Judge Perry raises a quizzical eyebrow. Wolfe shrugs, embarrassed.

The prosecution rests its case.

March 2, 1962

Rothman's lawyer Vincent Casey moves for a directed verdict. Showing that Rothman acquired slot machines from Mannarino for his Cuban operation is insufficient evidence, he protests, to prove Rothman's involvement in the alleged conspiracy.

The judge agrees. As to the government's attempt to show that Rothman was to cover a loan from a Swiss bank against the stolen Canadian bonds, the judge comments, "As far as I can see, the evidence appears to show only that the other defendants went to Rothman to borrow money from a friend."[5]

Judge Perry invokes a rarely used prerogative. He directs the jury to issue a verdict acquitting Rothman of the conspiracy charges. He orders Rothman to stay in Chicago, as he may be called as a defense witness. Vincent Casey and Rich Gorman congratulate Brad Eben. Even Rosden's lawyer shakes his hand. Eben is in a hurry to leave the courtroom; the television crews are waiting on the steps. Rothman flashes Wolfe thumbs-up on his way out.

Sunday, March 4, 1962

Fats Domino performs his signature tune "Blueberry Hill" on *The Ed Sullivan Show*.[6] Against Fats's steady piano, Wolfe mimes a solo on his air sax. Trudy is not in the mood. His mother had warned him, "At first, you can't stop looking at each other; later, you can't look each other in the eye."

Wolfe: When this is all over, we'll go to Florida.

Trudy: You can't blue sky your way out of this. Manion is going to put you away.

Wolfe: Gorman will fix the jury.

Trudy: They'll fuck you over, darling. Don't you get it? You're the fall guy.

She tosses back her drink, pours another.

Chicago, March 5, 1962

Since a defendant is not required to testify against himself, Wolfe and Mannarino never take the witness stand, avoiding the risks of cross-examination. For the record, they remain silent.

Their codefendant George Rosden testifies in his own defense, distancing himself from the others. He tells the jury he has a clear conscience. He makes a show of confessing—to being duped.

Rosden on the stand:

> *I believed that my client was the owner of the securities. First, he told me that the bonds were from his mother's estate in Canada. I advised him to make a clean breast of it to the Internal Revenue Service. But Rabin refused, because disclosure of the undeclared income would involve other persons. He said the interest and penalties on the undeclared income would kill him, and that was not a figure of speech! When I confronted him in my office, he told me the bonds were given to him by Castro supporters to buy weapons in Europe. What he told me first was just to hide the Cuba connection.*[7]

Wolfe: You self-serving sonofabitch!

Judge Perry raps his gavel at the outburst.

Gorman: During the course of these conversations with the Defendant Rabin, or at the time that you were in the office of the FBI in

Washington, D.C., did it come to your knowledge that Mr. Rabin's statement was that he had received these bonds from a person by the name of Garcia?

Rosden: Yes.

Gorman: Did Mr. Rabin tell you that the purpose of his obtaining these bonds was to make a trip to Europe for the purpose of paying for arms that had been purchased?

Rosden: No. The bonds he talked about were supposed to be bonds that he received as payment or collateral payment for his services.

Gorman: And did he tell you what services he was to perform?

Rosden: He did.

Gorman: And what were those services?

Rosden: He told me that he was supposed to pay and make shipment arrangements to pay for arms for Castroites in Cuba—to pay not in Cuba but to pay in Europe.

Gorman: In connection with this meeting in New York, where you said that you had a conversation with Rabin in connection with a payment that was to be made and you say you assumed he was waiting for a messenger from Canada, that is only an assumption on your part, is that correct?

Rosden: No, he mentioned a messenger, if I recall, he mentioned a messenger who would bring him money but he didn't mention the name and from whom the messenger was coming.

Gorman: But there is no doubt in your mind so far as you are concerned that he did tell you that he received these bonds from Cuban interests?

Rosden: Yes, he told me that on first of November 1958.

Wolfe: That *momser*[8] is killing me.

March 12, 1962

Don Manion is disturbed by Rothman's acquittal. Did the syndicate have something on Judge Perry? Or one of the jurors? He needs to think clearly. The idealistic young district attorney crafts his soliloquy. He rehearses the prosecution's closing argument at home in front of a mirror.

He plays to the courtroom.

Manion: They were actors in an international drama, each man playing his vital role.

He walks toward the defense table. Mannarino, he says, was the source for the stolen bonds. He got the bonds from Cotroni, who is in prison in Quebec.

He turns to Rabin. His piercing blue eyes meet Wolfe's flinty stare. Neither blink.

Manion: Mannarino contacted Rabin, a jack-of-all-trades who had a lust for power and money.

Wolfe puts his hand to his mouth, hiding a smile at the description. Lust. Power. Money. The prosecutor steps to Rosden's table. Rabin, he charges, brought in Rosden, the lawyer with entrée to international finance.

Passionate and righteous, Manion faces the jury. He gestures toward the three remaining defendants.

Manion: These men are examples of daring and deceit with utter contempt for the laws under which we all live.[9]

He urges the jury to convict Wolfe, Mannarino, and Rosden on all counts.

The defense lawyers jostle to be first with their rebuttals. They defer to Mannarino's lawyer Vincent Casey, the most senior. The acerbic Casey attacks Manion's conspiracy narrative.

Casey: What was spun was a great international intrigue, but it was nothing but a spiderweb, not strong enough to hold the government evidence. The prosecution has not proved that my client was linked to Rabin's activities in Europe.

Rosden's defense is that his client Wolfe deceived him into thinking that the bonds were valid. His lawyer pleads that the German not be held criminally responsible for a "mistake in judgment."[10]

Gorman steps to the plate for Wolfe. Indignant, he claims there is no evidence to prove his client knew the bonds he pledged at Credit Suisse were stolen.

> Gorman: And when my client learned of the bonds' dubious background, he attempted to make restitution to the Swiss. Knowledge of the alleged crime is an essential element, and that hasn't been proven.

> *Since* guilty knowledge is a state of mind *and it is not possible to look into a man's mind to see what goes on in there, the only way you have of determining guilty knowledge is for you to take into consideration all of the facts and circumstances in this case as shown by the evidence including the exhibits, and determining whether the defendants knew the bonds were stolen at the times in question. — Instructions to the jury, no. 25*[11]

Judge Perry warns the jurors that they had better tell their families that they might be coming home late or not at all.

The conference table in the jury room is strewn with evidence. Fourteen volumes of transcripts totaling more than 4,000 pages of testimony. Ashtrays overflow. The coffee is stale. The jury works until 11:00 p.m., when they are taken to a nearby hotel to be sequestered for the night.

Wolfe's Dream
Somewhere in the Caribbean

Wolfe and Trudy enjoy tropical cocktails on the deck of a yacht. Everyone is on board. His brother Leon and his wife Val, his brother Milton and Sheila, his sister Beryl, the Bette Davis doppelgänger. Sam Mannarino. Casino owner Norman Rothman and Olga Chaviano. Kent Tomlinson and Dollye. Fergus, the Black foreman. Meyer Lansky. Stella. All congratulate Wolfe.

Wolfe slides his arm around Trudy, escorts her to the railing. They scan the blue-green sea, an ocean of blue and green bonds, millions and millions and millions of dollars in bonds, stretching to the horizon. As the camera pulls back . . .

Credits begin to scroll across the screen. A Wolfe Rabin Production.

Wolfe rolls onto his side, awakened by a flash of lights through the window. What an extraordinarily vivid dream. He begins steeling himself for the day in court. He looks at Trudy, sleeping beside him, reaches an arm to pull her close.

Chicago, March 13, 1962

By noon of the second day of deliberations, a consensus develops that Rosden was a dupe. Some say he's still culpable. But when the foreman polls the jury, the vote is unanimous: not guilty on all counts. Strike two against Manion and the prosecution's conspiracy case.

Figure 12.1. Sam Mannarino on the telephone, 1962. Sam Mannarino calls his wife to report that he has been acquitted, Chicago, March 13, 1962. PHOTO UPI.

The jury turns to Mannarino and the counts against him. The discussion runs barely an hour. The jury accepts the testimony that Mannarino's trips to Canada were for hunting and fishing. They find no evidence to connect him to the bond scheme. The vote is unanimous on the first poll.

On learning of the not-guilty verdict, Mannarino races to the pay phone. A wire service photographer captures Sam calling his wife with news of his acquittal. Strike three for the prosecution. District attorney Don Manion faces the reporters, his conspiracy case in a shambles.

March 14, 1962

Judge Perry threatens to declare the jury deadlocked if it fails to reach a verdict on Wolfe's guilt or innocence by 11:00 p.m.

The jury must now decide Wolfe's fate. Steam radiators hiss, the jury room is stuffy and hot. Someone opens a window, and icy gusts clear the air. The debate over Wolfe's guilt or innocence heats up.

The bonds were in his drawer.

Someone could have put them there.

He flew the bonds from Canada.

No proof of that.

He tried to pay back the Swiss.

He clipped the coupons.

But he didn't cash them.

Rabin didn't hurt anybody.

Banks have insurance.

Since all the charges against Rothman, Mannarino, and Rosden have been dismissed, there is no conspiracy. Wolfe is consequently found innocent of charges of concealing stolen bonds, wire fraud, and conspiracy to dispose of stolen bonds.

Chicago, March 14, 1962

The jury must still decide on the four counts of trading bonds Wolfe allegedly knew to have been stolen. After hours of deliberation, the foreman calls for a vote. One by one, he polls the seven women and four other men around the table in the smoke-filled room. One by one, the jurors make their choices until only the foreman is left to cast his vote. The verdict must be unanimous.

In the courtroom, the foreman addresses the judge. Since Mannarino, Rothman, and Rosden were all acquitted, there was no conspiracy.

Manion has a sinking feeling. The case is falling apart before his eyes.

Confirmed when the foreman announces that the government failed to prove all the overt acts alleged in the wire fraud charge against Wolfe.

One indictment after another, the jury declares Wolfe not guilty on counts five through nine. Wolfe shakes Gorman's hand.

The foreman continues. Since there cannot be a conspiracy of one, the jury has decided that the bond disposal plot was a one-man operation conducted by Rabin.

"We, the jury, find the defendant William W. Rabin guilty as charged in count 1 of the indictment . . ."

Fear spikes through Wolfe's central nervous system.

Figure 12.2. William Rabin, left, with lawyer Richard Gorman, after guilty verdict, March 14, 1962. COURTESY OF CHICAGO HISTORY MUSEUM STM-037010479, PHOTO BY RALPH WATERS/*CHICAGO SUN-TIMES*.

"... guilty as charged in count 2 of the indictment."

This isn't happening.

The jury finds Wolfe guilty on four counts of pledging stolen bonds at Central National Bank. Wolfe faces a maximum sentence of ten years in prison and a $10,000 fine on each count. He will continue to be free on bond for two weeks, when Judge Perry will pronounce sentence.

Gorman claps Wolfe on the shoulder. You're not going to prison. Trust me.

When the proceedings conclude, Wolfe leaves the courtroom, Gorman trailing to his left. The flash pops on a Speed-Graphic, capturing the moment. Wolfe looks drawn and stressed. The photographer asks Wolfe to remove his hat. A second flash, this shot a close-up, Wolfe with hat in his hands. His eyes cannot conceal his pain.

Chicago, March 30, 1962

Wolfe stands facing the bench as Judge Perry pronounces sentence. He responds stoically to fines that total $40,000. He stiffens when the judge sentences him to ten years in the federal penitentiary. He turns to look in the back of the courtroom for Trudy. Wan and pale, she grips Leon's hand, her knuckles white. Wolfe had insisted his wife and brother keep their distance during the trial, not to get tarnished by association. They have come over his objections. Leon puts his arm around Trudy, holds her tight.

Wolfe will be released on bond of $50,000 pending appeal. He has the weekend to get the money or go to prison.

Morden, Manitoba, March 1962

An Oldsmobile with Illinois plates traverses a two-lane highway across the frozen plains. Slows past a sign at the edge of town—"Morden, Capital of the Corn and Apple Belt, population 2,500."

The Olds parks in the center of town, across the street from a two-story wood frame building that looks like the set for a western. The sign on the establishment reads "Rabinovitch Bros, Haberdashers."

When Wolfe left Morden in 1927, Doc Rabinovitch bought this building for his two younger sons to start their own business. But Leon soon followed Wolfe to Chicago. Milton ran the store but never changed the name on the sign. Milt is a popular man in town, chairman of the Chamber of Commerce, master of the Masonic lodge, general manager of the junior hockey team. With a son and twin daughters, he enjoys a comfortable, bucolic lifestyle, a universe apart from Wolfe's high-octane pursuit of the American dream in Chicago.

A black man graying at the temples, Fergus, enters the store, looks around at the displays of work clothes, racks of outerwear, fine suitings, shirts, and accessories. Milt emerges from the shoe department, sees the stranger, extends his hand. As they shake, the stranger puts his thumb on the space between Milt's second and third knuckles, pressing hard. A secret Masonic handshake.

Milt looks him in the eye. A flicker of recognition. The foreman from the jukebox factory.

Fergus: Brother Wolfe sent me.

Milt: All the way from Chicago?

Fergus: —in a blizzard.

Milt asks him to wait. He goes to his office at the back of the store, slides his chair up to a four-foot-high steel safe. By the rote of a lifetime, he spins the lock three to the right, two to the left, three to the right. The tumblers fall into place. He opens the heavy door, reaches into the safe to remove a small cashbox, black with maroon and gold trim. He opens the lock on the box, removes the fifty $1,000 bills that Wolfe had given him to keep "for a rainy day." A wistful expression crosses his face as he counts the money, then slides the bills into an envelope. He returns the box to the safe, closes the door, and spins the lock.

At the sales counter, Milt hands Fergus the envelope. This must be what you came for. He invites the stranger to stay for dinner but is politely declined. Perhaps another time.

Milt calls to the eleven-year-old boy playing in the corner by the thread boxes. David! Come here. Come meet Uncle Wolfe's friend from Chicago. I had been watching, frozen in my place. We had never seen an African American in Morden. As the only Jewish family in a town of Anglo-Saxons and Mennonites, we were the sole minority.

Wolfe makes bail. Gorman files notice that he will appeal the verdict.

Leechburg, Pennsylvania, May 25, 1962

With his not-guilty verdict in the bonds case, Sam Mannarino decides to ingratiate himself with law enforcement. He calls the Pittsburgh office of the FBI. At Mannarino's Bonfire Restaurant, the racketeer unburdens himself to agent Tom Forsyth in an extraordinary interview.

"Wolfe Rabin," he tells the agent, "has his conviction on appeal, and he should win. Wolfe is a shrewd operator and a clever businessman; he's given Sam good advice on many legitimate deals.

"Norman Rothman never cheated on him, he always keeps his word. He has done a lot for the government, by which I mean the CIA. He's got a lot of friends in Cuba, we would never have sent any guns to Castro. We knew from the beginning that Castro was a Commie, we had to help Batista but he didn't up a good fight."

Agent Forsyth asks him how the guns were taken from the armory. Smiling, Mannarino says, "You leave the door open at an armory tomorrow, and I will take the guns out."

Forsyth: Would you have taken a plea deal in the bonds case?

Mannarino: I wudda been willing to take a two-year rap anytime to save the nine weeks of aggravation of that trial. I could do two years vacation and be glad to get the rest.

He's got pithy words for Joe Merola. His only involvement was to fly to Pittsburgh with the pilot on the first trip north, he says. Merola's testimony as a government witness in Chicago had done Mannarino no harm, even though it was full of falsehoods. If Merola's testimony had sent him away, Sam says, then Merola would have to go, and the "family" would have to see to it.

Forsyth: Wasn't he made a member of the "family" thirty years ago?

Mannarino: He shudda been made a member of the cemetery thirty years ago!

Forsyth: Tell me about the "family." Is it true that "the door only swings one way and there is only one way to get out?"

Mannarino: Yeah. But if you know anything about the Masons, for example, they also take an oath to kill if it is necessary to get revenge. Ask Rabin, he's a Mason.

Forsyth: But it's true that Jews can't get into the family.

Mannarino: I dunno about that.

Forsyth: Meyer Lansky has a seat at the table, right?

Mannarino: Maybe the Jews have their own family, that's what I heard.

Forsyth: The Russian, Al Seid or Al Ross, he's a button man?

Mannarino laughs. "You're not from around here. You must be from New York. We don't call 'em that here."

Expansive, he launches into a reminiscence.

Mannarino: You know, in Miami, they refer to "button men" as "Elks." Years ago, when I went down there, I was approached by a deputy sheriff there who asked me to join the Elks club, which was just new then. He asked me to become a charter member. I told him, "You don't want me, I've got a record as long as your arm." And he told me, "We wouldn't have you if you didn't. That's what the club is made of here." I'm the number one Elk in the Miami area!

The agent asks if Mannarino's son-in-law Victor Carlucci is "earning his stripes" by serving his sentence in the guns case.

Forsyth: Will that get him into the New Kensington Mob?

Mannarino: If I had wanted to, I could have put him in the family a long time ago. That kid is going to go work legitimately when he gets out.

Waxing nostalgic, Mannarino refers to his mother as the most influential person in his life.

Mannarino: You know what she told me? She said, "If you are going to do something, do it by yourself. Otherwise, there will always be a witness."

The conversation goes into the night, covering Mannarino's proposed land developments, his business reverses, his gas well interest, his investment in a new coin-operated vending machine, his opposition to traffic in narcotics, and his relationship with his secretary.

When the meeting breaks up, Mannarino reminds the agent that he hasn't said anything. And he will be glad to sit down under the same conditions anytime.

Agent Forsyth notes in his report that *subject should be considered armed and dangerous.*[12]

The FBI continues to stalk Mannarino's clubs and businesses. But it will be the Internal Revenue Service that ultimately takes him down.

Chicago, July 13, 1962

Wolfe opens the door to an apartment at the Essex House. He sets down his valise and attaché case and calls to Trudy. He hears the needle scratching at the end of a record, over and over. He calls for Trudy again. No response.

Wolfe walks to the bedroom. He sees Trudy curled up on the bed, calls to her. It's me. He sits on the bed, touches her shoulder.

She is not breathing. Pill bottles litter the bed and nightstand. Wolfe's face turns white. He holds her lifeless body, sobbing endlessly.

An ambulance siren sounds in the distance. Cruiser lights flash through the window from the street below. The room is swarming with police and paramedics. But it is too late. The needle still scratches at the end of a record. Wolfe walks over to the turntable, lifts the arm, removes the disc. Ella Fitzgerald. "Cry Me a River."

A detective interviews the hotel manager, who tells him that Mrs. Rabin had acted strangely in recent weeks and had told a number of people she intended to kill herself.[13]

Wolfe goes on a bender. Trudy's death tears him apart. How could he have not seen it coming? She had always been there, watching out for him, urging him forward, plucky, comforting. He had been so self-absorbed, at such a price.

Leon and Val take him in and dry him out. They are relieved when the coroner's inquest exonerates him.

January 1963

In his relentless pursuit of organized crime, Robert Kennedy, now attorney general of the United States, determines to put Sam Mannarino behind bars. He orders the FBI to install wiretaps at Mannarino's scrapyard, his coin machine distributor, and the billiard room.

Joe Merola's prison term for gunrunning is commuted by President John F. Kennedy. The Department of Justice gives no reason for the commutation but notes that he has been of assistance to the government in other criminal investigations.[14] His release receives little notice, further supporting Mannarino's suspicion that Merola was an informer for the CIA.

The rush of events swirls around Wolfe. Gorman delays the appeal process as much as possible to keep Wolfe at liberty. A year after the guilty verdict, the Court of Appeal affirms the judgment of the lower court. The panel of judges notes that "the defendant's trips to Montreal afford reasonable basis for the jury to infer that such bonds were being brought from Canada to Chicago for disposition—a movement in interstate and foreign commerce" and that the defendant's actions "warranted a reasonable inference that defendant was aware of the stolen character of the securities he pledged in Chicago."[15]

Gorman makes one last desperate play. He requests that the Supreme Court hold an appeal hearing. The legal delays buy Wolfe another six months. But the Court denies the request, and he finally must face the reality of going to prison.

Terre Haute, Indiana, November 1, 1963

Leon and Wolfe drive along the chain-link and barbed-wire perimeter of the Federal Correctional Institute on the outskirts of Terre Haute, Indiana. It is a new type of prison, not the penitentiary of old, a medium-security facility for white-collar criminals.

About to get out of the car, Wolfe turns to his brother.

Wolfe: It's a good thing Ma and Pa didn't live to see this.

Television news crews film Wolfe walking to the guardhouse. He turns and waves to the cameras.

Behind the bravado, he is engulfed by an overwhelming wave of remorse. He has embarrassed his brothers and lost his emotional center with Trudy.

His sister Ruby rides the bus all the way from Montreal to visit him. Wolfe's rumpled denim shirt falls loosely. He has lost weight in prison. Not his dapper self.

Ruby brings kasha knishes like Ma use to make. And a copy of a Canadian newsmagazine with a cover story on the inner workings of the crime cartel.[16] Profiling his international exploits, the reporter describes Wolfe as "an apple-cheeked, cane-carrying former Winnipegger."

"They would have bought me out of here," he tells his sister. "But it was better to do my time. Somebody had to take the fall."[17]

While Wolfe is on the inside:

- Sam Mannarino is convicted of tax fraud in the coin machine operation. He is sentenced to one year and one day and is paroled after six months.

- Norman Rothman is paroled in February 1965 after serving three and a half years on his conviction for gunrunning.

The Bureau of Prisons has no records of Wolfe's term in Terra Haute other than the certificate of parole.

Terre Haute, Indiana, August 1, 1966

Leon waits for Wolfe on his release. After thirty months in prison, Wolfe has slimmed down. The brothers embrace.

Cruising the interstate in Leon's new Pontiac, Wolfe takes out a notebook with pages of sketches. The color returns to his face. Full of excitement, he pitches Leon his concept for the satellite radio system he designed in the prison electrical shop. He looks up, catches the freeway sign. "Turn south," he orders. "I need to go to Houston."

Leon: Now?

Wolfe: I've got a meeting at NASA.

Leon is encouraged. With his ingenuity and unstoppable energy, Wolfe is back. Shoot the moon.

CODA

Technology and social change conspire to reduce the jukebox to a nostalgic device. The transistor radio, the Sony Walkman cassette player, and then compact disc players transformed music to personal choice rather than the drawing card bringing people together in public places. Chain restaurants displaced the bars, diners, and drive-ins that were the home for more than half a million jukeboxes across the United States. By the 1990s, the Rock-Ola Corporation was the only jukebox manufacturer remaining, with an output of just several hundred machines annually. In 2018, the iconic American brand was sold to foreign interests.

Wolfe died in 1967. There is no record of his death, no published obituary, no marker. When I asked my father how his brother died, a pained look crossed his face. He took his cigar from his mouth and responded stoically. "If you live the way he did, you'll die young too."

He went to the closet where he stored his coin collection and returned with a dollar bill in a see-through sleeve. It was a large Dominion of Canada banknote with a portrait of King George V in full beard and military regalia.

"When Wolfe left Morden in 1927," my father told me, "Ma gave him a dollar so he would never be broke. When Wolfe was dying, he gave it to Leon. And when Leon was dying, he gave it to me. This is the dollar Ma gave Wolfe. Now it's yours."

My father looked at me, his eyes watering. "He would have liked you."

Conclusion

AFTERWORD

IN THE COURSE OF MY RESEARCH, I SOUGHT TO INTERVIEW PARTICI-
pants and witnesses to Wolfe's escapades. There appeared to be no
living primary sources.

A lifelong telling of his brother's story by my father, Milton, who
passed away in 2001, became a touchstone for the narrative revealed in
the files. But other than two cousins who, as teenagers, briefly encountered Uncle Wolfe in the 1940s, there was no one to ask my growing
list of questions.

I had a series of near misses in my search for witnesses to Wolfe's life
and times. Four passed away while I was researching the story, before I
could contact them.

Donald Manion, the U.S. district attorney in the bonds case, lived in
Marin County, California, not far from my home for twenty years, until
his death in 2009 at age eighty-three.

Assistant district attorney Donald Atkins, author of the prosecution's
closing arguments in the bonds trial, died in Chicago in 2013 at age
eighty-one.

Leon's wife, my aunt Val, passed away in a Jewish nursing home in
Chicago in 2007 at the age of 103. A small envelope with her effects was
sent to a cousin in Winnipeg. It contained Leon's military decorations
and photographs with Leon, Wolfe, and my father Milton. I inquired if
there had been a key in the envelope of the kind that fits the lock on a
safety deposit box. "Nothing like that," I was told.

The release of more than 18,000 FBI files under the John F. Kennedy Assassination Records Act in 2017–2018 prompted me to reexamine the narrative of the "biggest bank robbery in the world" and the "largest money-laundering scheme in history." The files led me to the last living participant in the bonds caper, the femme fatale Dollye Tomlinson.

I located the former beauty queen, in her nineties, living in the same house that Kent had bought in 1959. Despite numerous attempts to reach her, I received no response.

I wrote an email to one of her sons, Jeff Tomlinson, explaining that I was a writer working on this book and would like to talk to his mother about a trial that his father Kent had testified in sixty years ago. I received a prompt reply that read, "Are you related to Bill Rabinovitch? Call me!"

I picked up the phone and explained that Wolfe was my father's brother. The voice in Florida replied with exuberance, "Uncle Bill was my favorite uncle! He used to carry me on his shoulders."

I explained again the purpose of my call and asked if Jeff had any memory of his father going to testify in a trial in Chicago. At first, it drew a blank; he was only three and a half years old at the time of the bonds trial. Then a memory was revived. "I remember Dad saying, 'I could go to jail. Don't ever tell the kids!'"

When he asked for more information, I shared several pages of the transcript of his father's testimony, which is in the public record. Jeff was thunderstruck. He had known his father as a larger-than-life character, flying around the country with his chicken pluckers and belief in UFOs, so Kent's involvement in a major criminal plot did not appear to him to be far-fetched.

Having no desire or intention to cause an emotional disturbance in a family that appeared to be ignorant of their father's and mother's escapades, I was cautious in revealing too much detail.

Her son was keen to go to the source. He patched his mother Dollye in on the call, explained who I was and that I and he had some questions for her. When I posed my first question, there was an awkward silence. Then Dollye replied, in an unmistakable South Texas twang.

"Wolfe was your father's friend," she said, speaking to her son.

"Dad told me he was a business consultant. He helps fix things."

Her son jumped in with a series of pointed questions.

Jeff: He went to Europe with you and Dad.

Dollye: I don't remember.

Jeff: He had some stolen bonds. Did they arrest him at our house?

Dollye: I don't remember.

Jeff: They called Dad to testify?

Dollye: I don't remember. You're asking me things I don't remember.

Jeff: Did you leave me and Billy with Ethel next door when you went to Europe?

Dollye: [Silence]

Jeff: I remember Dad said, "The mob could kill me for this."

Dollye: I never went to any trial, son. I didn't know what he was doing.

At this point, I determined that it was best to leave Dollye with her case of selective memory.

POSTSCRIPTS

Sam Mannarino died of a heart attack on June 5, 1967. He had just been deported from Canada after a hunting trip in Alberta.

Norman "Roughhouse" Rothman was convicted in New York in 1972 for unlawful transportation of stolen securities. He was sentenced to five years in prison. A year later, he pleaded guilty to income tax evasion in Florida.[1] Rothman's conviction for gun smuggling was vacated in 1975 because Rothman was not informed that his codefendant Joe Merola, with whom he shared counsel, was an informant for the FBI and CIA.[2]

Giuseppe "Pep" Cotroni was released from prison in 1971. He died of cancer in 1979 at age fifty-seven.

Joe Merola began serving a one-year sentence for petty larceny in New York City in November 1972.[3] Two years later, he was indicted by a Los Angeles County grand jury for stock manipulation and fraud. In December 1976, a Chicago newspaper reported that Merola had received more than $50,000 in 1975 for furnishing information to the Illinois Bureau of Investigation.[4]

Al Seid, the hit man who was contracted to "dispose of" Wolfe Rabin, was convicted of extortion on June 24, 1965. He disappeared later that night, and his body was found on his lawyer's farm. Seid was the "torch man" and enforcer for the Mannarino organization and was scheduled to stand trial on a charge of firebombing a shopping center. It was believed that he was murdered to prevent his implicating the other parties to the arson.[5]

Richard Gorman, Wolfe's lawyer, was convicted of income tax evasion in 1968. After spending less than one day in jail, he was released by an order from Supreme Court Justice Thurgood Marshall when the Court learned that eavesdropping devices were used to obtain the mob lawyer's conviction. Gorman later served two years in prison on the tax evasion charges.

Assistant district attorney Donald Manion moved to California in 1968 and was appointed administrative law judge for the Social Security Administration.

Olga Chaviano, the fiery entertainer and wife of Norman Rothman, escaped from Cuba to Miami in 1966. An energetic performer, she staged a career comeback with dance spectaculars in Las Vegas and New York, costarring with her son Faustino Rothman. Her performing career ended with Faustino's death in 1997.

Leon Rabinovitch died of emphysema in 1969 at age fifty-eight.

Dollye Tomlinson assumed control of the rubber chicken plucker business following Kent's death in 1991 and continued to run the company until her ninetieth birthday. In the 1970s, her career as a mature model blossomed, and she was featured in *Vogue* magazine.

Bonds from the Brockville Savings heist continued to circulate throughout the global banking system for the next twenty-five years. The bonds surfaced in Switzerland, Central and South America, New York, Miami, Toronto, and Hong Kong.[6]

Wolfe's deepest secret would emerge after I completed the draft of this book. A submission to the website Ancestry.com yielded a supposedly distant cousin with an Italian surname who had entered Wolfe Rabinovitch in his family tree as his great-grandfather. His great-grandmother was the artist Stella Atkins.

In 1930, Stella gave birth to the child Wolfe sired, a baby girl she named Yvette. The girl was my first cousin. Stella soon married a prominent attorney, Michael Lamperti, and had two more children with him. Michael was the only father Yvette ever knew.

When she was dying, Stella gave her daughter a manila envelope full of old letters and clippings. Yvette put it away but never opened the envelope.

When Yvette, the cousin I never knew, passed away in 2016, one of her daughters found and opened the envelope her grandmother had left. It contained a few short letters from Wolfe, dated 1930, and yellowed clippings from the Chicago newspapers about his arrest in 1959 and the trial that followed.

Wolfe's secret had been kept for ninety years. His daughter Yvette had married at seventeen and had five children—a whole branch of extended family I look forward to getting to know. After all, there is *something* in our DNA.

Acknowledgments

I had long been challenged to research Wolfe's life, but many details were concealed as he had intended. Key to shedding light on his exploits were the transcripts of the trials he was involved in. For her dedication in locating physical copies of the transcripts, I am grateful to Betty Furimsky of the National Archives and Records Administration office in Chicago.

Through funeral home records for Bernice Filben, I connected with descendants of the jukebox inventor William Filben. I spoke with his granddaughter Mary Quinn, who generously shared family memorabilia.

I visited the operations of the Rock-Ola Corporation in Torrance, California, the last remaining jukebox manufacturer in the United States. Glenn Streeter, who acquired the company from founder David Rocko-la's family in 1992, is an inventor and designer himself in the tradition of the jukebox pioneers. In addition to examining the collection of histori-cally significant coin machines and other cultural artifacts, I was granted access to the company's archive of the numerous litigations to which Rock-Ola was party.

For her assistance in developing this book, I offer thanks to my daughter Zara, who researched and compiled a detailed time line of the true events and provided insightful editorial comment. In keeping with the family memoir aspect of this project, I am grateful to my sister Sandra Rabinovitch, producer of CBC Radio's *Writers & Company*, for unlocking Pandora's box when she submitted to a website for DNA analysis. This led to the discovery of Wolfe's girlfriend Stella, his secret child, and his grandchildren. Thank you also to my sister Celia Rabinovitch, artist and writer, for her support and passion for our family's history and the restoration of the photograph by Nick Yudell of Wolfe's stunt on the telephone pole.

I am indebted to my friends Dennis McIntosh, a veteran television journalist, who offered notes on an early draft, and Larry Danielson, a teacher who has inspired generations of students, for his critical edit of an early version of the manuscript.

My thanks also to my literary agent Diane Nine, who was fascinated by Wolfe's story and guided the project to publication.

Finally, to my wife and life partner Marsha Karr, who lived through every new discovery of Wolfe's exploits, my gratitude for her undying support, advice, and encouragement for all my endeavors.

Notes

Cast of Characters

1. U.S. Department of the Treasury, Bureau of Narcotics, *Mafia: The Government's Secret File on Organized Crime* (New York: Skyhorse Publishing, 2009).

Preface

1. Jefferson Morley and Rex Bradford, "Federal Agencies Face April Deadline on Secret JFK Files," JustSecurity.org, April 20, 2021, www.justsecurity.org/75795/federal-agencies-face-april-deadline-on-secret-jfk-files.

Chapter One

1. Yiddish, "village."

2. Gdansk, Poland.

3. Ruby (Rabinovitch) Freygood, "Swinging on the Gate" (unpublished manuscript), typescript.

4. Yiddish, "kosher butcher."

5. My grandmother called of her children by their Yiddish names—Hana, Aaron, Rivka, Velvyl, Mehel, Leibl, and Beryl.

6. Inspired by a scene from *Angels with Dirty Faces*, directed by Michael Curtiz (Warner Bros., 1938).

7. Hermann Gruber, "Masonry (Freemasonry)," *The Catholic Encyclopedia*, vol. 9 (New York: Robert Appleton Company, 1910), accessed June 1, 2022, www.newadvent.org/cathen/09771a.htm.

8. Yiddish, literally, "compassion."

9. Virden, 150 miles northwest of Morden.

10. Andrew Clayman, "Rock-ola Mfg Corp, est. 1927," Made in Chicago Museum, www.madeinchicagomuseum.com/single-post/rock-ola.

11. Clayman, "Rock-ola Mfg Corp."

12. John Bollinger, "I'm Walking, Yes, Indeed, but Not Talking: The Great 1929 Slot Machine Scandal," *American Mafia* (blog), April 2006, www.americanmafia.com/Feature_Articles_348.html.

13. Bollinger, "I'm Walking."

14. Clayman, "Rock-ola Mfg Corp."

15. Bollinger, "I'm Walking."

16. I have changed her name in respect for the privacy of her family.

17. Seventy years later, old-timers recalled that Milt had the first car radio in southern Manitoba. Vic Burgess had accompanied Milton on the road trip to Chicago. Vic Burgess, conversation with author, Winnipeg, Manitoba, June 2001.

18. Bollinger, "I'm Walking."

19. Inspired by a scene in *The Public Enemy*, directed by William A. Wellman (Warner Bros., 1931).

CHAPTER TWO

1. U.S. President, Proclamation, "National Jukebox Week, 1988," Proclamation 5896 of November 3, 1988, Ronald Reagan Presidential Library and Museum, www.reaganlibrary.gov/archives/speech/proclamation-5896-national-jukebox-week-1988.

2. "Five Years for Glass; Manager of San Francisco Phone Company Sentenced for Bribery," *New York Times*, September 5, 1907.

3. U.S. Congress, House of Representatives, Committee on the Judiciary, *To Provide for Recordings in Coin-Operated Machines at a Fixed Royalty Rate: Hearings before Subcommittee No. 2 of the Committee on the Judiciary, House of Representatives*, 82nd Cong., 2nd sess., on H.R. 5473, February 7, 1952.

4. U.S. Congress, House, Committee, *To Provide for Recordings*.

5. Lewis Nichols, "The Ubiquitous Jukebox," *New York Times*, October 5, 1941.

6. "Mints' Output Up; Demand Still Heavy," *Billboard*, October 26, 1940.

7. "The Evolution of the Jukebox: Top 15 Moments in Jukebox History," *Rockbot* (blog), April 2014, https://blog.rockbot.com/the-evolution-of-the-jukebox-top-15-moments-in-jukebox-history.

8. Theodore Pratt, "Land of the Jook," *Saturday Evening Post*, April 26, 1941.

9. "Juke or Jook Joints?," uDiscoverMusic.com, June 10, 2012, www.udiscovermusic.com/stories/blues-juke-or-jook-joints.

10. *Juke Girl*, directed by Curtis Bernhardt (Warner Bros., 1942).

11. Bosley Crowther, "'Juke Girl,' a Tumbled Melodrama about Florida Vegetable Growers, Opens at the Strand," *New York Times*, June 20, 1942.

12. Bruce N. Canfield, "Making a Different Kind of Music," *American Rifleman*, April 2008.

13. Eleanor Jewett, "Water Colors Show Leaves Art Institute," *Chicago Tribune*, August 30, 1942.

14. My father preserved Leon's letters from the front in a box of Cuban panetelas. All mail to Sergeant Leon Rabinovitch of the 230th Signals Corps went through army censors in San Francisco. Milton numbered and dated the letters. Although the collection is incomplete, the highest number is seventy-six.

15. "A Million Is a Lot of Anything," *Billboard*, May 1946.

16. Tony Soprano could not have been created without the real-life Sam Mannarino and others like him. An analysis of social mobility among a generation born to

mostly Italian immigrants can be found in Jeanine Mazak-Kahne, "Small-Town Mafia: Organized Crime in New Kensington, Pennsylvania," *Pennsylvania History: A Journal of Mid-Atlantic Studies* 78, no. 4 (2011): 363.

17. "Small Ideas Have Large Commercial Possibilities," *Modern Mechanix & Invention*, May 1936.

18. A seven-day period of ritual mourning.

19. "Mr. Siegel Make It Legal," written by Jack Yellen, lyrics reprinted courtesy of Jack Yellen Music.

20. Beryl (Rabinovitch) Burtnick, untitled memoirs, unpublished manuscript, typescript.

21. "Lefty Korman" is a composite character. The character's dialogue is taken from testimony before the McClellan Committee. U.S. Congress, Senate, Select Committee on Improper Activities in the Labor or Management Field, *Investigation of Improper Activities in the Labor or Management Field: Hearings before the Select Committee on Improper Activities in the Labor or Management Field*, 85th Cong., 2nd sess., 1958, and 86th Cong., 1st sess., 1959.

22. U.S. Congress, Senate, Select Committee, *Investigation of Improper Activities*, 16,511.

CHAPTER THREE

1. To further muddy the waters, Mannarino's syndicate incorporated a separate sales company named the National Filben Corporation, which had offices in the same building on South Wabash as Wolfe's company, the Filben Manufacturing Company.

2. David Rockola, testimony, *Rock-ola Manufacturing v. Filben Manufacturing*, No. 13,695 Civil (8th Cir. App. 1948).

3. "Slain Juke Racket Rival Feared Bomb," *Chicago Tribune*, October 26, 1961.

4. Gus Russo, *The Outfit: The Role of Chicago's Underworld in the Shaping of Modern America* (New York: Bloomsbury, 2003), 190.

5. Gert Almind, "Batavia Metal Products Co., Illinois," American Jukebox History, October 24, 2010, www.jukeboxhistory.info/filben/history/batavia_metal_products.pdf.

6. "And while [the Maestro] was displayed in Chicago, those people booked $42 million worth of orders on the display of the model." Leonard Baskfield, testimony, *Rock-ola Manufacturing v. Filben Manufacturing*, No. 13,695 Civil (8th Cir. App. 1948), 101.

7. "Filben Music Line Output Reaches Peak," *Billboard*, October 4, 1947, 106.

8. Capehart wrote and delivered variations of the same speech over several years. See Homer E. Capehart, "Americanism and Music," *Billboard*, July 27, 1940, and Kerry Seg-rave, *Jukeboxes: An American Social History* (Jefferson, NC: McFarland, 2002).

9. "After the war, when Homer Earl Capehart had become senator . . . the Packard company was revived and headed by the founder's son, Thomas Capehart, and the jukebox series Packard 7 Pla-Mor (pronounced play more) and Packard Manhattan with matching speakers was produced until the spring of 1949. The Packard Manufacturing Company was taken over by The Rudolph WurliTzer Company early in September, 1951." Gert J. Almind, "The History of Coin-Operated Phonographs," unpublished manuscript, November 8, 2010, www.jukeboxhistory.info/packard/history.html.

10. William B. Pickett, "The Capehart Cornfield Conference and the Election of 1938: Homer E. Capehart's Entry into Politics," *Indiana Magazine of History* 73, no. 4 (December 1977): 251–75, www.jstor.org/stable/27790239.

11. William B. Pickett, "Homer E. Capehart: Phonograph Entrepreneur," *Indiana Magazine of History* 82, no. 3 (September 1986): 264–76, www.jstor.org/stable/27790996.

12. "The Capehart," *Fortune*, February 1941.

13. "The Great Cornfield Conference," Indiana Public Media, October 10, 2011, https://indianapublicmedia.org/momentofindianahistory/great-cornfield-conference.

14. "The Great Cornfield Conference."

15. Pickett, "The Capehart Cornfield Conference."

16. Homer E. Capehart, "Dealing with the Relief Problem," Capehart Manuscripts, August 27, 1938 (Indiana State Library, Indianapolis).

17. "Capehart to Host GOP," *Billboard*, August 20, 1938, 66.

18. Greenberg's contract was worth $80,000.

19. Segrave, *Jukeboxes*, 128.

20. "Rock-Ola Files 8 Patent Infringement Suits vs. Filben; Latter in Appeal," *Billboard*, October 16, 1948.

21. Deposition of William W. Rabin, February 17, 1949, *Rock-ola Manufacturing Corporation v. Filben Corporation* (N.D. Ill. 1949).

22. Collectors today prize the Maestro as "one of the rarest (if not the rarest) of all jukeboxes. The Maestro stands out like a shining beacon." See "Juke Box Epilogue," Jitterbuzz.com, 2011, www.jitterbuzz.com/jukeboxes_conclusions.html.

23. Robert Kennedy, *The Enemy Within* (New York: Harper & Bros., 1960), 302.

CHAPTER FOUR

1. Bob Greene, "Juke Box: Mobsters Play the Tune," *Newsday*, June 6, 1955.

2. Amy A. Kisil, "Tommy James Sinito AKA The Chinaman: The Early Years, Part 1," AmericanMafia.com, February 2007, www.americanmafia.com/Feature_Articles_377.html.

3. U.S. Congress, House of Representatives, Committee on the Judiciary, *To Provide for Recordings in Coin-Operated Machines at a Fixed Royalty Rate: Hearing before Subcommittee No. 3 of the Committee on the Judiciary, House of Representatives*, 82nd Cong., 1st–2nd sess., on H.R. 5473, 1951–1952.

4. U.S. Congress, House of Representatives, Committee, *To Provide for Recordings*.

5. Greene, "Juke Box."

6. "Lansky-Smith New Wurlitzer N.Y., N.J. Conn. Distribs.," *Billboard*, March 13, 1943, 59.

7. U.S. Congress, Senate, Special Committee to Investigate Organized Crime in Interstate Commerce, *Investigation of Organized Crime in Interstate Commerce: Hearings before a Special Committee to Investigate Organized Crime in Interstate Commerce*, 81st Cong., 2nd sess., and 82nd Cong., 1st sess., pursuant to S. Res. 202, Part 7 New York–New Jersey, 1950–1951, 1579.

8. U.S. Congress, Senate, Special Committee, *Investigation of Organized Crime*.

9. U.S. Congress, Senate, Committee, *Investigation of Improper Activities*, 16,511–16,512.

10. U.S. Congress, Senate, Committee, *Investigation of Improper Activities*, 16,512.

11. U.S. Congress, Senate, Committee, *Investigation of Improper Activities*, 16,512.

12. U.S. Congress, Senate, Committee, *Investigation of Improper Activities*, 16,834.

13. Kennedy, *The Enemy Within*, 247.

14. U.S. Congress, Senate, Committee, *Investigation of Improper Activities*, 16,514–16,515.

15. U.S. Congress, Senate, Committee, *Investigation of Improper Activities*, 16,539.

16. Kennedy, *The Enemy Within*, 302.

CHAPTER FIVE

1. Much of the information about Wolfe, the Mannarinos, and their associates comes from reports made by the FBI or the CIA agents tracking them. These records are located in the President John F. Kennedy Assassination Records Collection at the National Archives and Records Administration (NARA) (www.archives.gov/research/jfk). References to FBI or CIA records within this collection begin (at first appearance) with administrative information, such as reporting agent and report subject, date of the record creation, and then "JFK NARA," followed by the FBI record number and page number, where applicable; subsequent references to the same source will have administrative information with the FBI record number in parentheses. This reference system for these records follows that established in Jeanine Mazak-Kahne, "Small-Town Mafia: Organized Crime in New Kensington, Pennsylvania," *Pennsylvania History: A Journal of Mid-Atlantic Studies* 78, no. 4 (2011): 355–92. Report of Thomas G. Forsyth, June 25, 1959, JFK NARA, 124-10283-10057, A.

2. Built in 1951, the Biltmore Terrace was a fine example of Miami modernism by the noted hotel architect Morris Lapidus. Despite protests by historic preservationists, the hotel was demolished in 2015.

3. Report of MM, December 24, 1959, JFK NARA, 124-10213-10447, 6.

4. Rothman is the basis for the character Ben "The Butcher" Stein in the Starz television series *Magic City*, written and produced by Mitch Glazer (2010).

5. Yiddish, "a brute."

6. Report of MM (124-10213-10447), 3.

7. Dr. Cappy Rothman graduated from the University of Miami School of Medicine, specializing in urology. He became a male fertility specialist and founded the Center for Male Reproductive Medicine in Los Angeles and the California Cryobank, the world's largest sperm bank. For more information, see www.malereproduction.com/about-cmrm/dr-cappy-rothman.

8. Report of PG on Joseph Raymond Merola and Stuart Sutor, July 16, 1959, JFK NARA, 124-90100-10199.

9. Ernest Havemann, "Mobsters Move in on Troubled Havana and Split Rich Gambling Profits with Batista," *Life*, March 10, 1958.

10. Yiddish, generally a compliment about a person who has mental agility—as some would put it, "a head on his/her shoulders."

11. This passage is based on the testimony of Sergeant Leslie Sterritt, Brockville Police Department, in *United States v. Rabin*, No. 13804 (7th Cir. 1962).

12. Raymond Daniell, "$2,240,000 Stolen in Bank in Canada; Vault in Brockville Cracked—Negotiable Paper Taken—Suspect Is Seized," *New York Times*, May 6, 1958.

13. "Bank Loot Total Rises; Canadian Safecrackers' Haul Put as High as $10,000,000," *New York Times*, May 8, 1958.

14. Bigger even than the notorious Brink's armored car robbery in Boston in 1950.

15. The break-in at Brockville Trust imitates the French crime film *Rififi*. In the film's compelling centerpiece, a gang of thieves cuts through the ceiling of a jewelry store from the apartment above. The critic for the *Los Angeles Times* called it a "master class in breaking and entering as well as filmmaking." Directed by blacklisted American Jules Dassin, the film won the award for best director at the 1955 Cannes Film Festival and played to large audiences during its Montreal release. Kenneth Turan, "Rififi Remains the Perfect Heist (Movie)," *Los Angeles Times*, October 6, 2000.

16. Vince Johnson, "Mannarino Mob Flies High," *Pittsburgh Post-Gazette*, May 23, 1958.

17. "Sam Made Woods Turn Too Short!," *Pittsburgh Post-Gazette*, November 27, 1957.

18. U.S. Department of the Treasury, Bureau of Narcotics, *Mafia: The Government's Secret File on Organized Crime* (New York: Skyhorse Publishing, 2009).

19. Jane Bradbury Lord, "UFOs in the Desert," *Hi-Desert Magazine*, Summer 1991.

20. "Joe Merola was at his best when working as a finger man and especially where he worked in this respect in setting up automobile dealers. Merola would contact used car dealers in South Carolina or other distant points and advise them that they could purchase six or ten automobiles cheap at the automobile auctions in Pennsylvania. These dealers feeling that they had an inside tip would come to Pittsburgh with cash and Joe Merola would steer them to the Cadillac Hotel where they would later be robbed before going to the auction." Robert High Daniels, ex-con and Merola accomplice, in report of PG on Joseph Raymond Merola and Stuart Sutor, February 12, 1959, JFK NARA, 124-90100-10105, 32.

21. Memorandum of Justin F. Gleichauf on Joseph Merola, February 8, 1961, JFK NARA, 104-10124-10214.

22. Report of PG, August 23, 1961, JFK NARA, 124-10283-10157.

23. In Quebec and Newfoundland up to 1968, there was no divorce law. The only way for an individual to get divorced in these provinces was to apply to the federal Parliament for a private bill of divorce. These bills were handled primarily by the Senate of Canada, where a special committee would undertake an investigation of a request for a divorce. If the committee found that the request had merit, the marriage would be dissolved by an Act of Parliament. Canada, Parliament of Canada, *Acts of the Parliament of Canada (21st Parl., 1st sess., c. 43)*, 1949, https://archive.org/details/actsofparl1949v02cana_0/page/n17/mode/2up.

24. Report of PG (124-90100-10105), I.

25. *United States v. Rabin*, No. 13804 (7th Cir. 1962).

CHAPTER SIX

1. Report of Edward Kinzer Jr., May 10, 1961, JFK NARA, 124-10280-10185, 10.

2. Report of Edward Kinzer Jr. (124-10280-10185), 9.

3. "Raid of Canton, Ohio, National Guard Armory," *Associated Press*, October 14, 1958.

4. "Armory Raid Laid to Cuban Rebel Sympathizers," *Marysville Journal-Tribune*, October 15, 1958.

5. Report of PG on Joseph Raymond Merola and Stuart Sutor, October 23, 1959, JFK NARA, 124-90100-10286, I. In the same report, Sam Mannarino is implicated in the gun deal: "Considerable background information was furnished to the Newark office pointing to the possibility that Colle could have met Pittsburgh national top hoodlum Sam Mannarino in Washington, D.C."

6. Report of Edward Kinzer Jr. (124-10280-10185), 10.

7. Pronounced *loy*.

8. Peter Eavis, "The List That Big Banks Don't Wish to Be On," *New York Times*, November 1, 2012, https://dealbook.nytimes.com/2012/11/01/the-list-that-big-banks-dont-wish-to-be-on.

9. Report of PG on Joseph Raymond Merola and Stuart Sutor (124-90100-10199), 4.

10. Report of PG, August 23, 1961, JFK NARA, 124-10283-10164, 13.

CHAPTER SEVEN

1. "Seized Arms, Said Stolen from Armory," *Morgantown Post*, November 5, 1958.

2. "Seized Arms Linked to Alleged Racketeer."

3. Report of Edward Kinzer Jr. (124-10280-10185), 51.

4. U.S. Congress, Senate, Committee, *Investigation of Improper*, 16,512.

5. U.S. Congress, Senate, Committee, *Investigation of Improper*, 16,512.

6. "The True Life of Rebel Castro," *GENTE* (American Edition), January 5, 1958, 34.

7. W.W. Johnson, U.S. Department of the Treasury to Commissioner of Investigations, U.S. Bureau of Customs, March 27, 1958, in Cuban Information Archives, document 0288, https://cuban-exile.com/doc_276-300/doc0288.html.

8. T. J. English, *Havana Nocturne: How the Mob Owned Cuba . . . and Then Lost It to the Revolution* (New York: HarperCollins, 2008), 305.

9. English, *Havana Nocturne*, 305–6.

10. Report of Edward Kinzer Jr. (124-10280-10185), 14.

11. Report of PG on Joseph Raymond Merola and Stuart Sutor (124-90100-10105), G.

CHAPTER EIGHT

1. Evan Thomas, *Robert Kennedy: His Life* (New York: Simon & Schuster, 2002).

2. U.S. Congress, Senate, Committee, *Investigation of Improper*, 16,598.

3. Report of Edward Kinzer Jr. (124-10280-10185), 49–50.

4. George Rosden, testimony, *United States v. Rabin*, No. 13804 (7th Cir. 1962), 332.

5. Report of Edward Kinzer Jr. (124-10280-10185), 19–20.

6. "Took Stolen Bonds as Fee, Rabin Claims," *Chicago Daily Tribune*, February 15, 1959.

7. Report of CG on Joseph Raymond Merola and Stuart Sutor, April 30, 1959, JFK NARA, 124-90100-10167, 4.

8. "Took Stolen Bonds."

9. "How Mystery Man Goofed Perfect Crime," *Chicago Tribune*, July 4, 1959; "Big Shot Financier's Blunder Exposed $8.5 Million Theft," *St. Louis Globe-Democrat*, July 5, 1959.

10. Report of Edward Kinzer Jr. (124-10280-10185), 25.

11. Report of PG, July 29, 1959, JFK NARA, 124-10216-10402, 2–3.

12. Report of Edward Kinzer Jr. (124-10280-10185), 44.

13. "International Gang Believed Involved in $10 Million Theft," *Port Angeles Evening News*, March 4, 1959.

14. Report of Edward Kinzer Jr. (124-10280-10185), 52.

15. "Shields Face from Camera," *Uniontown Morning Herald*, March 19, 1959.

16. Report of Richard Gordon Douce, May 4, 1959, JFK NARA, 124-10283-10052, 2.

17. Report of Edward Kinzer Jr. (124-10280-10185), 21–23.

CHAPTER NINE

1. The conversation between Cotroni and the informant and undercover agent is based on trial transcripts, as quoted in Peter Edwards, *Blood Brothers: How Canada's Most Powerful Mafia Family Runs Its Business* (Toronto: McLelland-Bantam, 1990), 33–34.

2. Report of CG (124-90100-10167), 7.

3. Report of John P. Lenihan, January 4, 1960, JFK NARA, 124-10280-10177, 36.

4. Report of Edward Kinzer Jr. (124-10280-10185), 26.

5. Report of Edward Kinzer Jr. (124-10280-10185), 42–43.

6. Report of John P. Lenihan (124-10280-10177), 36–38.

7. Report of John P. Lenihan (124-10280-10177), 38.

8. Mannarino describes his arrest file. Report of PG, February 23, 1962, JFK NARA, 124-10278-10041, 3.

9. "World's Biggest Burglary Solved," *Tucson Daily Citizen*, July 3, 1959.

10. Edwards, *Blood Brothers*, 36.

11. Corporal punishment was legal in Canada until 1972.

12. Report of PG on Joseph Raymond Merola and Stuart Sutor, July 31, 1959, JFK NARA, 124-90100-10230, 51.

13. Report of PG, July 29, 1959, JFK NARA, 124-10216-10402.

14. Report of PG (124-10216-10402).

15. Report of John P. Lenihan (124-10280-10177), I.

16. Report of John P. Lenihan (124-10280-10177), 45–46.

17. *United States v. Carlucci*, 288 F.2d 691 (3d Cir. 1961).

18. Mannarino was interviewed by FBI special agent John S. Portella, excerpted in Michael Canfield and Alan Weberman, *Coup d'Etat in America: The CIA and the Assassination of John F. Kennedy* (San Francisco: Quick American Archive, 1992), 64.

19. Canfield and Weberman, *Coup d'Etat*, 74.

20. Report of Richard Gordon Douce, October 2, 1958, JFK NARA, 124-10216-10348, 40.

21. Report of PG, August 23, 1961, JFK NARA, 1124-10283-10157, 10.

22. Report of MM on Joseph Raymond Merola, September 28, 1960, JFK NARA, 124-90110-10027, 6.

23. Report of MM on Joseph Raymond Merola (124-90110-10027), 6.

24. "Rabin allegedly has available some kind of fictitious government agency credentials (which he will use) to approach an unidentified individual who has in his possession allegedly over a million dollars in $10,000 denominations. They will request the bills be turned over to them and in turn will give what appears to be a valid receipt." Report of MM on Joseph Raymond Merola (124-90110-10027), 6.

CHAPTER TEN

1. David E. Scheim, *Contract on America: The Mafia Murder of President John F. Kennedy* (New York: Zebra, 1989), 386.

2. Ovid Demaris, *Captive City: Chicago in Chains* (New York: Lyle Stuart, Inc., 1969), 309–16.

3. Scheim, *Contract on America*, 386.

4. Canfield and Weber, *Coup d'Etat*, 76.

5. Rothman approached an agent of the CIA with a plan to seize two Russian MiG aircraft from Cuba. "Rothman claimed he could induce the defection of a Czech pilot and a Cuban who would fly the MIGs to the U.S. When queried re his motive, Rothman frankly stated he could not perform these services for the U.S. if he was serving time in jail, referring to his Pittsburgh conviction on conspiracy to transport stolen guns in interstate commerce." Canfield and Weber, *Coup d'Etat*, 74.

6. "October 7, 1960 Debate Transcript," Commission on Presidential Debates, accessed June 3, 2022, www.debates.org/voter-education/debate-transcripts/october-7-1960-debate-transcript.

7. Report of Thomas G. Forsyth, February 27, 1961, JFK NARA, 124-10283-10073, 3–4.

8. Report of Thomas G. Forsyth (124-10283-10073), 4.

9. Memorandum of Justin F. Gleichauf on Joseph Merola (104-10124-10214).

10. Report of PG, June 26, 1961, JFK NARA, 124-10216-10495, 1.

11. Report of MM, July 21, 1961, JFK NARA, 124-10289-10376, 1–2.

12. Report of PG (124-10283-10157), 4.

13. Report of PG (124-10283-10157), 4.

14. Report of FBI Headquarters to Assistant Attorney General Herbert J. Miller, August 22, 1961, JFK NARA, 124-90101-10044, 1.

15. *United States v. Rabin*, No. 13804 (7th Cir. 1962).

CHAPTER ELEVEN

1. Broadcast live on WGN-TV Chicago and the Dumont network, 1950–1954.

2. "FOP Plays Smart," *Simpson's Leader-Times*, January 24, 1962.

3. "Perry Rips Likely Jurors for Prejudicial Attitude," *Chicago Daily Tribune*, January 20, 1962.

4. This chapter is drawn from the Transcript of Proceedings in *United States v. Rabin*, No. 13804 (7th Cir. 1962).

5. "Scienter" is a legal term that refers to intent or knowledge of wrongdoing. This means that an offending party has knowledge of the "wrongness" of an act or event prior to committing it.

6. Curiously, Eddie Lawton Smith's testimony, ordered stricken, remains in the printed record in its entirety.

Chapter Twelve

1. Report of PG, February 23, 1962, JFK NARA, 124-10278-10041.

2. *United States v. Rabin*, No. 13804 (7th Cir. 1962).

3. "Brockville Bonds Used by Cubans?," *Ottawa Journal*, March 7, 1962.

4. *United States v. Rabin*, No. 13804 (7th Cir. 1962).

5. *United States v. Rabin*, No. 13804 (7th Cir. 1962).

6. *The Ed Sullivan Show*, watched by more than one-third of the American audience on Sunday evenings on CBS, had an exceptional lineup on March 4, 1962: Elizabeth Ashley, Art Carney, Wilt Chamberlain, Phyllis Diller, Troy Donahue, Paula Prentiss, Connie Stevens, Henny Youngman, and Fats Domino.

7. "Mannarino Jury Hears Defendant," *Indiana Evening Gazette*, March 6, 1962.

8. Yiddish, "bastard."

9. "Jury Weighing Bank Loot Case," *Bridgeport Post*, March 13, 1962.

10. "Jury Weighing."

11. *United States v. Rabin*, No. 13804 (7th Cir. 1962).

12. Report of Thomas G. Forsyth, June 29, 1962, JFK NARA, 124-10286-10001.

13. "Wife in Stolen Bond Inquiry Found Dead," *Chicago Tribune*, July 14, 1962.

14. "Herbert J. Miller, Jr., Assistant Attorney General, Criminal Division, U.S. Department of Justice by memorandum dated April 26, 1962, referred to Joseph Merola and advised that on April 13, 1962, a petition for executive clemency, together with his recommendation that petition be granted, was forwarded to pardon attorney Reed Cozart." Canfield and Weber, *Coup d'Etat*, 85.

15. *United States v. Rabin*, No. 13804 (7th Cir. 1962).

16. Alan Philips, "Inner Workings of the Crime Cartel," *Maclean's*, October 5, 1963.

17. Oral history related by Steven Freygood, interview with the author, 2014.

Conclusion

1. Canfield and Weberman, *Coup d'Etat in America*, 78.

2. Canfield and Weberman, *Coup d'Etat*, 78.

3. Canfield and Weberman, *Coup d'Etat*, 71.

4. Canfield and Weberman, *Coup d'Etat*, 78.

5. Clifford Karchmer and Douglas Little, *Report on Organized Crime* (Harrisburg: Commonwealth of Pennsylvania, Department of Justice, Pennsylvania Crime Commission, July 2, 1970), 61, www.academia.edu/40228290/Pennsylvania_Crime_Commission_The_Report_on_Organized_Crime_by_Special_Agents_Clifford_Karchmer_and_Douglas_Little.

6. Dennis Stein, "The Great Heist of '58," *The Fine Print* (blog), February 13, 2011, http://thefineprints.blogspot.com/2011/02/great-heist-of-58-bydennis-stein-cool.html.

Bibliography

"A Million Is a Lot of Anything." *Billboard*, May 1946.

Almind, Gert. "Batavia Metal Products Co., Illinois." American Jukebox History, October 24, 2010. www.jukeboxhistory.info/filben/history/batavia_metal_products.pdf.

———. "The History of Coin-Operated Phonographs." Unpublished manuscript, November 8, 2010. www.jukeboxhistory.info/packard/history.html.

"Armory Raid Laid to Cuban Rebel Sympathizers." *Marysville Journal-Tribune*, October 15, 1958.

"Bank Loot Total Rises; Canadian Safecrackers' Haul Put as High as $10,000,000." *New York Times*, May 8, 1958.

"Big Shot Financier's Blunder Exposed $8.5 Million Theft." *St. Louis Globe-Democrat*, July 5, 1959.

Bollinger, John. "I'm Walking, Yes, Indeed, but Not Talking: The Great 1929 Slot Machine Scandal." *American Mafia* (blog), April 2006. www.americanmafia.com/Feature_Articles_348.html.

Burtnick, Beryl (Rabinovitch). Untitled memoirs. Unpublished manuscript, typescript.

Canada. Parliament of Canada. *Acts of the Parliament of Canada (21st Parl., 1st sess., c. 43)*, 1949. https://archive.org/details/actsofparl1949v02cana_0/page/n17/mode/2up.

Canfield, Bruce N. "Making a Different Kind of Music." *American Rifleman*, April 2008.

Canfield, Michael, and Alan Weberman. *Coup d'Etat in America: The CIA and the Assassination of John F. Kennedy*. San Francisco: Quick American Archive, 1992.

Capehart, Homer E. "Dealing with the Relief Problem." Capehart Manuscripts, August 27, 1938, Indianapolis: Indiana State Library.

———. "Americanism and Music." *Billboard*, July 27, 1940.

"Capehart to Host GOP." *Billboard*, August 20, 1938.

Clayman, Andrew. "Rock-ola Mfg Corp, est. 1927." Made in Chicago Museum. www.madeinchicagomuseum.com/single-post/rock-ola.

Crowther, Bosley. "'Juke Girl,' a Tumbled Melodrama about Florida Vegetable Growers, Opens at the Strand." *New York Times*, June 20, 1942.

Daniell, Raymond. "$2,240,000 Stolen in Bank in Canada; Vault in Brockville Cracked—Negotiable Paper Taken—Suspect Is Seized." *New York Times*, May 6, 1958.

Demaris, Ovid. *Captive City: Chicago in Chains*. New York: Lyle Stuart, Inc., 1969.

Eavis, Peter. "The List That Big Banks Don't Wish to Be On." *New York Times*, November 1, 2012.

Edwards, Peter. *Blood Brothers, How Canada's Most Powerful Mafia Family Runs Its Business*. Toronto: McLelland-Bantam, 1990.

English, T. J. *Havana Nocturne: How the Mob Owned Cuba . . . and Then Lost It to the Revolution*. New York: HarperCollins, 2008.

"Filben Music Line Output Reaches Peak." *Billboard*, October 4, 1947.

"Five Years for Glass.; Manager of San Francisco Phone Company Sentenced for Bribery." *New York Times*, September 5, 1907.

"FOP Plays Smart." *Simpson's Leader-Times*, January 24, 1962.

Freygood, Ruby (Rabinovitch). "Swinging on the Gate." Unpublished manuscript, typescript.

Greene, Bob. "Juke Box: Mobsters Play the Tune." *Newsday*, June 6, 1955.

Gruber, Hermann. "Masonry (Freemasonry)." *The Catholic Encyclopedia*. Vol. 9. New York: Robert Appleton Company, 1910. Accessed June 1, 2022. www.newadvent.org /cathen/09771a.htm.

Havemann, Ernest. "Mobsters Move in on Troubled Havana and Split Rich Gambling Profits with Batista." *Life*, March 10, 1958.

"Held by FBI in 2.4 Million Theft." *Chicago Tribune*, February 14, 1959.

"How Mystery Man Goofed Perfect Crime." *Chicago Tribune*, July 4, 1959.

"International Gang Believed Involved in $10 Million Theft." *Port Angeles Evening News*, March 4, 1959.

Jewett, Eleanor. "Water Colors Show Leaves Art Institute." *Chicago Tribune*, August 30, 1942.

Johnson, Vince. "Mannarino Mob Flies High." *Pittsburgh Post-Gazette*, May 23, 1958.

Johnson, W. W. U.S. Department of the Treasury to Commissioner of Investigations. U.S. Bureau of Customs, March 27, 1958. Cuban Information Archives, document 0288. https://cuban-exile.com/doc_276-300/doc0288.html.

"Juke Box Epilogue." Jitterbuzz.com, 2011. www.jitterbuzz.com/jukeboxes_conclusions. html.

"Juke or Jook Joints?" uDiscoverMusic.com, June 10, 2012. www.udiscovermusic.com /stories/blues-juke-or-jook-joints.

"Jury Weighing Bank Loot Case." *Bridgeport Post*, March 13, 1962.

Karchmer, Clifford, and Douglas Little. *Report on Organized Crime*. Harrisburg: Commonwealth of Pennsylvania, Department of Justice, Pennsylvania Crime Commission, July 2, 1970. www.academia.edu/40228290/Pennsylvania_Crime _Commission_The_Report_on_Organized_Crime_by_Special_Agents_Clifford _Karchmer_and_Douglas_Little.

Kennedy, Robert. *The Enemy Within*. New York: Harper & Bros., 1960.

Kisil, Amy A. "Tommy James Sinito AKA The Chinaman: The Early Years, Part 1." AmericanMafia.com, February 2007. www.americanmafia.com/Feature _Articles_377.html.

"Lansky-Smith New Wurlitzer N.Y., N.J. Conn. Distribs." *Billboard*, March 13, 1943.

Lord, Jane Bradbury, "UFOs in the Desert," *Hi-Desert Magazine*, Summer 1991.

"Mannarino Jury Hears Defendant." *Indiana Evening Gazette*, March 6, 1962.

Mazak-Kahne, Jeanine. "Small-Town Mafia: Organized Crime in New Kensington, Pennsylvania." *Pennsylvania History: A Journal of Mid-Atlantic Studies* 78, no. 4 (2011): 355–92.

Memorandum of Justin F. Gleichauf on Joseph Merola, February 8, 1961, JFK NARA, 104-10124-10214.

"Mints' Output Up; Demand Still Heavy." *Billboard*, October 26, 1940.

Morley, Jefferson, and Rex Bradford. "Federal Agencies Face April Deadline on Secret JFK Files." JustSecurity.org, April 20, 2021. www.justsecurity.org/75795/federal -agencies-face-april-deadline-on-secret-jfk-files.

Nichols, Lewis. "The Ubiquitous Jukebox." *New York Times*, October 5, 1941.

"October 7, 1960 Debate Transcript." Commission on Presidential Debates. Accessed June 3, 2022. www.debates.org/voter-education/debate-transcripts/october-7 -1960-debate-transcript.

"Perry Rips Likely Jurors for Prejudicial Attitude." *Chicago Daily Tribune*, January 20, 1962.

Philips, Alan. "Inner Workings of the Crime Cartel." *Maclean's*, October 5, 1963.

Pickett, William B. "The Capehart Cornfield Conference and the Election of 1938: Homer E. Capehart's Entry into Politics." *Indiana Magazine of History* 73, no. 4 (December 1977): 251–75. www.jstor.org/stable/27790239.

———. "Homer E. Capehart: Phonograph Entrepreneur." *Indiana Magazine of History* 82, no. 3 (September 1986): 264–76. www.jstor.org/stable/27790996.

Pratt, Theodore. "Land of the Juke." *Saturday Evening Post*, April 26, 1941.

"Raid of Canton, Ohio, National Guard Armory." *Associated Press*, October 14, 1958.

Report of CG on Joseph Raymond Merola and Stuart Sutor. April 30, 1959. JFK NARA. 124-90100-10167.

Report of Edward Kinzer Jr. May 10, 1961. JFK NARA. 124-10280-10185.

Report of FBI Headquarters to Assistant Attorney General Herbert J. Miller. August 22, 1961. JFK NARA. 124-90101-10044.

Report of John P. Lenihan. January 4, 1960. JFK NARA. 124-10280-10177.

Report of MM. December 24, 1959. JFK NARA. 124-10213-10447.

———. July 21, 1961. JFK NARA. 124-10289-10376.

Report of MM on Joseph Raymond Merola. September 28, 1960. JFK NARA. 124-90110-10027.

Report of PG. July 29, 1959. JFK NARA. 124-10216-10402.

———. June 26, 1961. JFK NARA. 124-10216-10495.

———. August 23, 1961. JFK NARA. 124-10283-10157.

———. August 23, 1961. JFK NARA. 124-10283-10164.

———. February 23, 1962. JFK NARA. 124-10278-10041.

Report of PG on Joseph Raymond Merola and Stuart Sutor. February 12, 1959. JFK NARA. 124-90100-10105.

———. July 16, 1959. JFK NARA. 124-90100-10199.

———. July 31, 1959, JFK NARA. 124-90100-10230.

———. October 23, 1959. JFK NARA. 124-90100-10286.

Report of Richard Gordon Douce. October 2, 1958. JFK NARA. 124-10216-10348, 40.

———. May 4, 1959. JFK NARA. 124-10283-10052.

Report of Thomas G. Forsyth. June 25, 1959. JFK NARA. 124-10283-10057.

———. February 27, 1961. JFK NARA. 124-10283-10073.

———. June 29, 1962. JFK NARA. 124-10286-10001.

"Rock-Ola Files 8 Patent Infringement Suits Vs. Filben; Latter in Appeal." *Billboard*, October 16, 1948.

Rock-ola Manufacturing v. Filben Manufacturing. No. 13,695 Civil (8th Cir. App. 1948).

Rock-ola Manufacturing Corporation v. Filben Corporation (N.D. Ill. 1949).

Russo, Gus. *The Outfit: The Role of Chicago's Underworld in the Shaping of Modern America.* New York: Bloomsbury, 2003.

"Sam Made Woods Turn Too Short!" *Pittsburgh Post-Gazette*, November 27, 1957.

Scheim, David E. *Contract on America: The Mafia Murder of President John F. Kennedy.* New York: Zebra, 1989.

Segrave, Kerry. *Jukeboxes: An American Social History.* Jefferson, NC: McFarland, 2002.

"Seized Arms Linked to Alleged Racketeer." *Morgantown Post*, November 6, 1958.

"Seized Arms, Said Stolen from Armory." *Morgantown Post*, November 5, 1958.

"Shields Face from Camera." *Uniontown Morning Herald*, March 19, 1959.

"Slain Juke Racket Rival Feared Bomb." *Chicago Tribune*, October 26, 1961.

"Small Ideas Have Large Commercial Possibilities." *Modern Mechanix & Invention*, May 1936.

Stein, Dennis. "The Great Heist of '58." *The Fine Print* (blog), February 13, 2011. http://thefineprints.blogspot.com/2011/02/great-heist-of-58-bydennis-stein-cool.html.

"The Capehart." *Fortune*, February 1941.

"The Evolution of the Jukebox: Top 15 Moments in Jukebox History." *Rockbot* (blog), April 2014. https://blog.rockbot.com/the-evolution-of-the-jukebox-top-15-moments-in-jukebox-history.

"The Great Cornfield Conference." Indiana Public Media, October 10, 2011. https://indianapublicmedia.org/momentofindianahistory/great-cornfield-conference.

"The True Life of Rebel Castro." *GENTE (American Edition)*, January 5, 1958.

Thomas, Evan. *Robert Kennedy: His Life.* New York: Simon & Schuster, 2002.

"Took Stolen Bonds as Fee, Rabin Claims." *Chicago Daily Tribune*, February 15, 1959.

Turan, Kenneth. "Rififi Remains the Perfect Heist (Movie)." *Los Angeles Times*, October 6, 2000.

U.S. Congress, House of Representatives, Committee on the Judiciary. *To Provide for Recordings in Coin-Operated Machines at a Fixed Royalty Rate: Hearings before Subcommittee No. 2 of the Committee on the Judiciary, House of Representatives.* 82nd Cong., 2nd sess., on H.R. 5473, February 7, 1952.

U.S. Congress, Senate, Select Committee on Improper Activities in the Labor or Management Field. *Investigation of Improper Activities in the Labor or Management Field: Hearings before the Select Committee on Improper Activities in the Labor or Management Field.* 85th Cong., 2nd sess., 1958, and 86th Cong., 1st sess., 1959.

U.S. Congress, Senate, Special Committee to Investigate Organized Crime in Interstate Commerce. *Investigation of Organized Crime in Interstate Commerce: Hearings before a Special Committee to Investigate Organized Crime in Interstate Commerce.* 81st Cong., 2nd sess., and 82nd Cong., 1st sess., pursuant to S. Res. 202, Part 7, New York-New Jersey, 1950–1951.

U.S. Department of the Treasury, Bureau of Narcotics. *Mafia: The Government's Secret File on Organized Crime.* New York: Skyhorse Publishing, 2009.

U.S. President. "National Jukebox Week, 1988." Proclamation 5896 of November 3, 1988. Ronald Reagan Presidential Library and Museum. www.reaganlibrary.gov /archives/speech/proclamation-5896-national-jukebox-week-1988.

United States v. Carlucci. 288 F.2d 691 (3d Circuit 1961).

United States v. Rabin. No. 13804 (7th Circ. 1962).

"Wife in Stolen Bond Inquiry Found Dead." *Chicago Tribune,* July 14, 1962.

"World's Biggest Burglary Solved." *Tucson Daily Citizen,* July 3, 1959.

Index

Hammergren, Milton "Mike":
in *Billboard*, 50; before
McClellan Committee, 55;
Whitefish Resort of, 36
Hanna, Al, 141
Hanna, Daniel "Speedo," 115, 116
Havana, Cuba: casinos in, 59–62,
100–102; Rothman, N., in,
62–63
heroin, G. Cotroni dealing, 119
high fidelity, of Continental Radio
Corporation, 52
de Hirsch, Baron, 1
Hoffa, James Earl, 133
Hoover, J. Edgar, 137
Hoyt, George: at Corydon
Travel Agency, 76; Manion
questioning, 152–53
Hudson's Bay Company
department store, Montreal,
73
Hughes, Howard, 1

Illinois. *See* Chicago, Illinois
Imperial Pawn Shop, Chicago, 57
Indiana: Cornfield Conference in,
41–42; Fort Wayne, 40; Terre
Haute, 175–77

Japan, Pearl Harbor attacked by, 20
John F. Kennedy Assassination
Records Collection Act
(2017), 180; Kinzer report in,
137
jukeboxes. *See* specific topics
Jukebox Wars, 34–35

Juke Girl (movie), 19
jury: Manion relation to, 143;
Perry relation to, 147–48, 162,
166

Kaplan, Arthur, 54
Kefauver, Estes: Eben relation to,
145; presidential run of, 51;
report to Congress of, 49–50
Kefauver Committee, 49; Lansky
testimony to, 50–51;
McClellan Committee
compared to, 54; on television,
xix
Kelly, Lehme, 55
Ken Iron and Steel Company, New
Kensington: Carlucci at, 93;
FBI at, 124
Kennedy, John F.: Bay of Pigs
action of, 136; Merola
sentence commuted by, 175;
Nixon debate with, 135;
presidential election of, 56.
See also John F. Kennedy
Assassination Records
Collection Act
Kennedy, Robert F.: as attorney
general, 175; Capehart, H.,
relation to, 48; on McClellan
Committee, xx, 54–56; Rabin,
G., reaction to, 105–6
Kiev, Ukraine, 1
Kinzer, Ed, Jr.: Rabin, W.,
interviewed by, 116;
report in John F. Kennedy
Assassination Records

radios, in cars: of M. Rabinovitch,
188n17; Rabin, W., design
for, 13
Raft, George, 100
RCMP. *See* Royal Canadian
Mounted Police
Reagan, Ronald: in *Juke Girl*, 19;
National Jukebox Week by, 17
Rek Chemical Company, Chicago,
78–79, 112–13, 146
Rififi (film), 192n15
Riggs Bank, Washington DC,
96–97
Riviera casino, Havana, 101
Rockola, David: Capehart, H.,
relation to, 48; at Century
of Progress Exposition,
13; Filben, W., relation to,
32–34; mechanized musical
instruments by, 18; at
Northwest Coin Machine
Show, 42; Rabin, W., relation
to, xix; slot machines of, 8–10
Rock-ola Company, 177; jukebox
machine parts of, 44; M1
rifles made by, 20–21, 33;
Model A jukebox of, 32
Rock-ola Model A jukebox, 32
Rockola Scale Company, 8
Rockola v. Filben, 33–34
Rondeau, Jean-Guy, 66–67
Rosden, George Eric: acquittal of,
167; arrest of, 124; in court,
140; Credit Suisse relation
to, 89, 108; FBI relation to,
96–97, 107, 109; Gorman

questioning, 163–64; Rabin,
W., met by, 82; Siegel
introduction by, 85–86;
von Stockar relation to, 88;
telegram from, 115; on trial,
147
Rothman, Cappy, 191n7
Rothman, Faustino, 61; career of,
182
Rothman, Norman "Roughhouse":
arrest of, 117, 123–24, 130;
Batista relation to, 62, 129,
172; Ben "The Butcher"
Stein based on, 191n4; at
Biltmore Terrace hotel,
58–59; Casey relation to,
162; casino connections of,
116; Chaviano relation to, 60,
61; conviction of, 181; during
Cuban revolution, 101–2;
Eben relation to, 145, 150–
51; in Havana, 62–63; jury
reaction to, 147; Lenihan
relation to, 114, 138–39;
Mannarino S., relation to, 99;
Merola relation to, 72; parole
of, 176; reaction to Castro,
134–35, 172; reaction to
communists in Cuba, 195n5;
Seid relation to, 136; on trial,
140–41; at Warwick Hotel,
110
Royal Canadian Mounted Police
(RCMP), 126; Cotroni, G.,
surveilled by, 75; FBI relation
to, 99

About the Author

David Rabinovitch is an Emmy, Peabody, and Gemini Award–winning filmmaker. Notable productions include *The Sultan's Women*, a docudrama revealing the true stories of an Ottoman princess and a woman leader of the Turkish revolution, both searching for love and freedom amid the turbulent last years of empire, and the landmark miniseries *Secret Files of the Inquisition*, which brought to life the stories of victims of intolerance, based on original research in European archives.

His significant films include the documentary *Politics of Poison*, which was screened for a congressional committee and resulted in the suspension of the domestic use of the chemical Agent Orange; *Shanghai Shadows*, the first American documentary in the People's Republic of China; and *Air Crash*, which exposed ambulance-chasing attorneys in the wake of a mass disaster and earned the Gavel Award of the American Bar Association.

He has filmed on five continents, and his productions have been broadcast in more than forty countries. He hails from the town of Morden, Manitoba, where his uncle Wolfe Rabin's exploits remain a subject of myth and lore.

He and his wife, artist Marsha Karr, live in Mercer Island, Washington, and in the *pueblo magico* of Todos Santos, Mexico. *Jukebox Empire: The Mob and the Dark Side of the American Dream* is his first book. For more information, visit www.davidrabinovitch.com.

PHOTO CREDIT: ZARA RABINOVITCH

PHOTO CREDIT: MELIKE ONAY